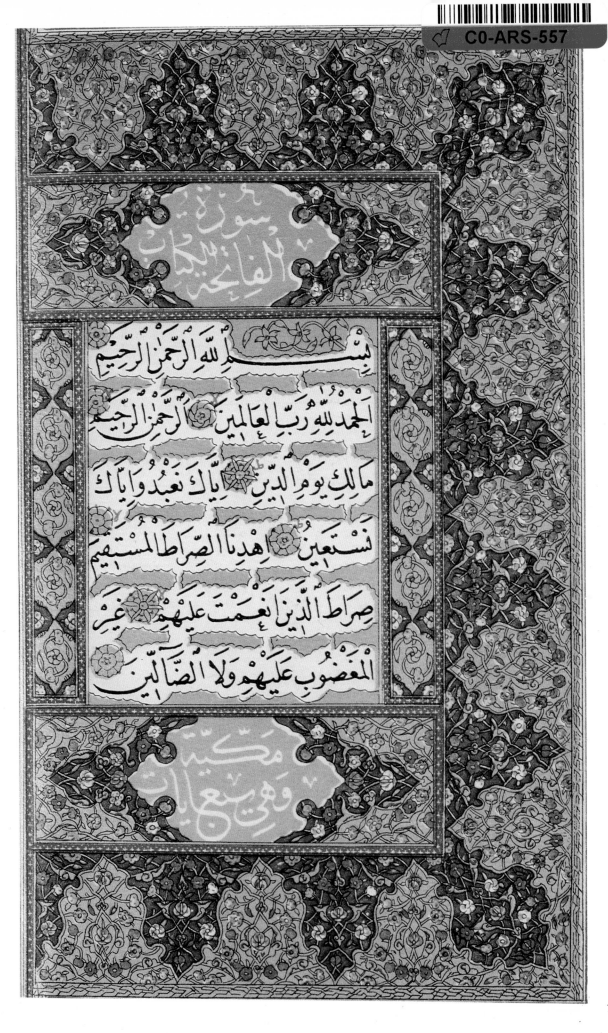

سورة الفاتحة والكتاب

بسم الله الرحمن الرحيم
الحمد لله رب العالمين ۝ الرحمن الرحيم
مالك يوم الدين ۝ اياك نعبد واياك
نستعين ۝ اهدنا الصراط المستقيم ۝
صراط الذين انعمت عليهم ۝ غير
المغضوب عليهم ولا الضالين

مكية
وهي سبع ايات

Preface

The purpose of this book is to convey to a non-Muslim audience an understanding of Islam, its history, culture, and contribution to civilization.

The mix of an easy-to-read text and visual representations including maps, charts, pictures, and drawings with informative captions explains the important message of Islam in a way that the reader will hopefully find thoughtful and appealing. Relevant verses of the *Qur'an* and sayings of the Prophet *(Hadith)* have been included where appropriate, as support for the narrative, and their interspersing sets out their relevant importance. The Arabic text of the *Qur'an* was also included because no translation can do it justice.

Most of the *Qur'an* quotes were translated by me in reliance upon several published translations, especially *The Holy Qur'an* translated by Abdullah Yusuf Ali (Khalil Al-Rawaf, 1946). My translation was done with a view to make the non-Arabic reader better understand the intended meaning.

This is both an informative and an artistic book which covers many aspects of Islam: religious, historical, geographic, social, legal, political, economic, cultural, scientific, and artistic. These aspects are dealt with in a way which at times may seem cursory but this does not forsake accuracy or depth.

The primary goal of this book is to inform those who know little or nothing about Islam and to enhance their understanding. As an educator that is all I can ask for, and as a Muslim, that is all I can aspire to. But as a member of the family of humankind I would feel gratified if this book can lead to a better understanding among peoples of the world and thus contribute to peace and harmony in our universe. Whether all or some of these expectations will be fulfilled is something the reader will have to judge.

M. Cherif Bassiouni

Chicago, September 1, 1988-H. 1409

Acknowledgements

The author gratefully acknowledges the support of the MidAmerica Arab Chamber of Commerce in connection with the cost of preparing the manuscript for publication, which was approved by its Board of Directors, and expresses his deep appreciation to Rand McNally Corporation of Chicago for publishing this book as a sign of their interest in the world of Islam.

Most of the illustrations contained in this book have been graciously provided by *Aramco World Magazine* and Rand McNally whose assistance in this respect was most useful.

In the selection of illustrations, their integration in the text and other ministerial functions, I was assisted by Olfat El-Mallakh of the MidAmerica Arab Chamber of Commerce to whom I express my appreciation as well as to Tom Malueg who edited an earlier version of the text, and appreciation to Alfred Polus for proofreading the final text. The design and layout of the book was done by John Wetzel whom I wish to thank, especially for his patience in redoing the layout repeatedly to produce this excellent result. My appreciation is also extended to Walid M. Shaar who did the calligraphy on the cover and the Qur'anic verse at the conclusion of the book, and to Dr. Shafiq Ismail who prepared the current map of the "Muslim world" (based on a map from the Chicago *Tribune*) and the "Distribution of the *Shia*" map. Specific acknowledgements for maps and illustrations appear in the text.

Finally, my appreciation to the American Arab Affairs Council (Washington, D.C.) for having published in 1985 an abbreviated text with the same title, which subsequently and with significant changes became this book.

Table of Contents

In The Beginning

It is estimated that there are over 900 million Muslims today. Many live in the Arab World (estimated at 120 million), but many more live in countries such as Iran, India, Pakistan, Bangladesh, Indonesia, the Philippines, Malaysia, China, the USSR, Nigeria, Cameroon, Chad, and Sudan. An estimated 3 million Muslims reside in the United States.

The world's three monotheistic faiths—Judaism, Christianity, and Islam—were born and developed in that small region called the Middle East. Abraham was born in the city of Ur, Mesopotamia (Iraq), some 1900 years before Jesus was born in Bethlehem (Palestine). Muhammad was born in Mecca (Saudi Arabia) in 570 A.D. Moses lived in Egypt, as did Jesus for a brief period in his infancy; Muhammad traveled throughout the Arabian Peninsula.

The Middle East straddles Africa and Asia Minor. It is bordered on the north from Turkey to Tunisia by the Mediterranean. To the south-east it is bordered by the Indian Ocean, which encircles the Arabian Peninsula, and to the east by the mountains of Iran and Turkey. To the west of Egypt lies the Sahara Desert. The races which inhabited these territories were the Semites, Hammites, Aryans, and the Indo-Europeans.

The Middle East region is the cradle of all the ancient civilizations. The oldest of these civilizations, the Egyptian, extended over five millenia. The fourth millennium B.C. witnessed the birth of the great civilizations along the Tigris-Euphrates valley (Turkey, Syria, Iraq). The Nile-centered Egpytian civilization was largely self-contained; those of the Tigris-Euphrates valley had more frequent contacts with other civilizations. As a result, they were periodically transformed as they came in contact with different cultures and peoples. The most important of these ancient civilizations were the Sumerian, Mesopotamian, Babylonian, Assyrian, Assyro-Babylonian, Aramean, Phoenician, Carthagenian, Canaanite, Hebrew, Philistine, Chaldean, Hurrian, Hittite, Kassite, and Mitani. Their peoples spoke a number of languages including Akkadian, Aramaic, Syriac, Sumerian, Hebrew (the language of the Torah), and Arabic (the language of the *Qur'an).*

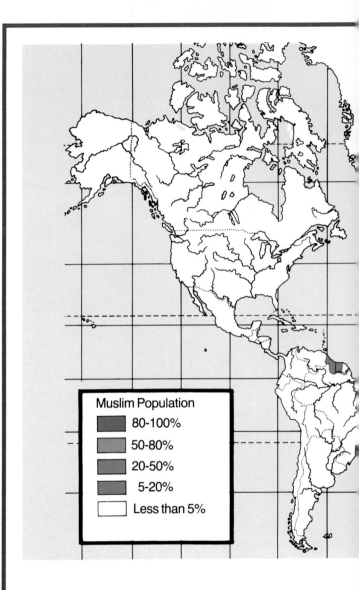

Muslim Population
- 80-100%
- 50-80%
- 20-50%
- 5-20%
- Less than 5%

Muslims constituted about 17% of the total world population in the year 1987.

Africa	245,111,000
Europe	8,902,000
Northern America	2,863,000
South Asia	547,350,000
East Asia	23,795,000
Latin America	645,000
Oceania	96,000
U.S.S.R.	31,807,000

Encyclopaedia Britannica: World Data

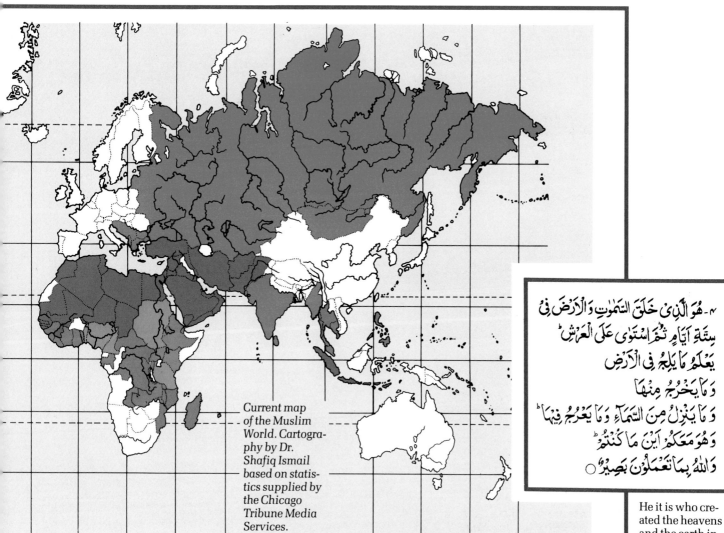

Current map of the Muslim World. Cartography by Dr. Shafiq Ismail based on statistics supplied by the Chicago Tribune Media Services.

Chicago Tribune Map; Sources: The World Factbook, Country Backgrounds.

Country	Total	Country	Total	Country	Total	Country	Total
Afghanistan	100%	Senegal	92%	Togo	50%	Bulgaria	13%
Bahrain	100%	South Yemen	91%	Ethiopia	40%	Yugoslavia	12%
Maldives	100%	Egypt	90%	Malaysia	38%	India	11%
Mauritania	100%	Indonesia	90%	Ghana	30%	Mozambique	10%
North Yemen	100%	Mali	90%	Guinea-Bissau	30%	Zaire	10%
Qatar	100%	Syria	90%	Sierra Leone	30%	Guyana	9%
Saudi Arabia	100%	United Arab Emirates	90%	Burkina Faso	25%	USSR	9%
Morocco	99.9%	Guinea	85%	Ivory Coast	25%	Sri Lanka	8%
Algeria	99%	Bangladesh	83%	Gabon	20%	Madagascar	7%
Kuwait	99%	Chad	80%	Israel and Palestine	20%	Trinidad & Tobago	6%
Somalia	99%	Comoro Islands	80%	Kenya	20%	Burma	5%
Tunisia	99%	Niger	80%	Liberia	20%	Philippines	5%
Iran	98%	Albania	70%	Malawi	20%	China	2.5%
Turkey	98%	Sudan	70%	Suriname	20%	Argentina	1%
Libya	97%	Brunei	60%	Uganda	20%	Bolivia	1%
Pakistan	97%	Lebanon	57%	Zambia	20%	Brazil	1%
Gambia	95%	Benin	50%	Cyprus	18%	Canada	1%
Iraq	95%	Cameroon	50%	Mauritius	17%	Colombia	1%
Jordan	95%	Nigeria	50%	Central African		United States	1%
Djibouti	94%	Tanzania	50%	Republic	15%	Mexico	.5%

> Proclaim! (or Read!) In the name of thy Lord and Cherisher, Who created—
>
> Created man, out of A (mere) clot of congealed blood:
>
> Proclaim! And thy Lord Is Most Bountiful,—
>
> He Who taught (The use of) the Pen…
> Qur'an 96:1-5

١- اِقْرَأْ بِاسْمِ رَبِّكَ الَّذِىْ خَلَقَ ۚ

٢- خَلَقَ الْإِنْسَانَ مِنْ عَلَقٍ ۚ

٣- اِقْرَأْ وَرَبُّكَ الْأَكْرَمُ ۙ

٤- الَّذِىْ عَلَّمَ بِالْقَلَمِ ۙ

In the first century B.C. the Greeks and then the Romans through conquest established their presence in the region. Then from the seventh to the eighteenth centuries A.D. the Arabs extended their presence to Europe and Asia. The ebb and flow of their conquests enriched the cultures with which they came in contact through the intermingling of peoples and the transfer of values and knowledge. The richness of Arab Islamic culture in the arts and sciences and the dissemination of Arab Islamic culture throughout the Mediterranean basin and Asia Minor and into Europe and portions of Asia and Africa has served to make it one of the foundations of today's civilizations.

Prophet Muhammad and the Birth of Islam

The word "Islam" is derived from the same root as the words *salaam* (peace) and *silm* (the condition of peace). Islam means to abandon oneself in peace. A Muslim, consequently, is one who in peace gives or surrenders himself or herself to God. Islam means accepting the faith freely—heart, mind, and soul. Surrendering to Islam, as a result, means giving oneself to belief without reservation, accepting the tenets of faith, and following both the letter and the spirit of the *Qur'an's* prescriptions.

Abraham, also called "The Patriarch," is the most important of the early prophets to the Jews, Christians, and Muslims. He founded, in what is now Mecca, the first temple in the world for the worship of a single god. He was also the father of Isma'il (Ishmael) and Ishaq

(Isaac). The descendants of Isaac ultimately formed what became the Hebrew tribes. The tribes of the Arabian Peninsula, the descendants of Isma'il, were the first people to become Muslims.

Until The 7th century the entire area of the Arabian Peninsula—bordered on the west by the Red Sea, on the east by the Arabian Gulf, on the south by the Indian Ocean and on the north by the Fertile Crescent (now Syria, Lebanon, Iraq, portions of Palestine and Jordan) —was inhabited for the most part by nomadic tribes. There were three Jewish tribes in Yathrib near Madina and others in Yemen. There were also a few Christians in the north and west of the Peninsula and in Yemen. Most of the inhabitants, however, were pagans.

Muhammad was known to meditate in the solitude of the desert. He frequently visited a cave called Hira just outside Mecca. During one of his meditations—he was 40 years old at the time—he received the first of his revelations from God. The *Qur'an* identifies the bearer of the message as the angel Gabriel, who commanded the Prophet Muhammad to read. When Muhammad responded that he didn't know how, Gabriel replied, "Read in the name of your Lord Who created man from a clot of blood…" In this way Muhammad became the bearer of the divine message.

In Islam there can be no confusion or doubt that Muhammad was a man, and only a man, chosen by the Creator to fulfill a divine mission as a prophet. Muhammad's mission was literally to "read" what *Allah* had ordered and ordained, nothing more. The Prophet received his revelations from God, sometimes in soli-

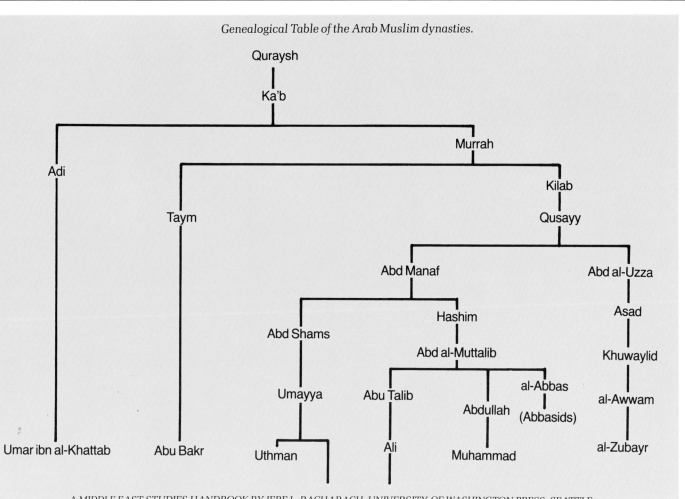

Genealogical Table of the Arab Muslim dynasties.

A MIDDLE EAST STUDIES HANDBOOK BY JERE L. BACHARACH, UNIVERSITY OF WASHINGTON PRESS, SEATTLE.

tude, sometimes in the presence of others. Words flowed from his mouth in a way that others described as inspired. This was Muhammad's *wahy* (divine inspiration or revelation). Muslims believe that the *Qur'an* is the Word of Allah expressed through the revelations to the Prophet.

Among the Arab tribes, the most powerful and noble was the Quraysh, into which Muhammad ibn 'Abd Allah ibn 'Abd al-Muttalib was born on Monday at dawn on the 12th of Rabi' Awal (the year 571 in the common era calendar). That year was known as the year of the Elephant—the year the Abyssinians invaded Mecca to destroy the Ka'ba. The year received its name from the fact that the army of the Abyssinians was supported by elephants!

According to tradition, the Prophet Muhammad is a direct descendent of Ishma'el, the son of Abraham. Muhammad's mission was presaged by the deliverance of his father, 'Abd Allah, after he had been chosen for sacrifice. The story is this. 'Abd Allah had nine

brothers, but he was the favorite son. His father 'Abd al-Muttalib was in charge of the well of the pilgrims. When the water of the well, Zamzam, dried up, he was at a loss as to what to do. He was advised to make offerings to the gods of one of his sons. Muhammad's father was chosen by lot. Reluctant to carry out the act, 'Abd Allah's father beseeched the pagan priests to spare his favorite son. They suggested that camels be offered in his stead. It took one hundred camels to satisfy the gods. The well filled again, and the life of 'Abd Allah was spared. This recalls the saying of the Prophet: "I am the son of the sacrificed...."

After his birth, as was the custom of the Arabs, Muhammad was given to a wet nurse, a nomad named Halimah as-Sa'diyah, to learn the ways of the desert early on in life. She recounted the following story about the Prophet. When the boy was four years old, two men dressed in white came, took the child, and removed something black from his chest. This story is often used to interpret Surah 94, Verses 1-3, of the *Qur'an*, which

Mosque of Ibn Tulun, showing courtyard, arcade, and minaret. Tulunid period, 876-9, at al-Qata'i', the new seat of government, north of Fustat, near Cairo, Egypt. (Rand McNally.)

reads: "Have we not Expanded thee thy breast?, And removed from thee thy burden, the which did gall Thy back?"

At the age six, Muhammad lost his mother, Aminah of the clan of az-Zuhrah. 'Abd al-Muttalib cared for him until the age of eight. His uncle, Abu Talib raised him, and taught him caravan trade after the death of his grandfather. Over the years Muhammad earned the name al-Amin—the honest—for his rare qualities of character.

The history of the Prophet, his deeds and sayings, were at first memorized by his companions and passed on as oral record. They were first comprehensively recorded by the historian Ishaq ibn Yasar (ca. 768). Later the deeds and sayings of the Prophet (the *Hadith*), the circumstances surrounding their occurrence, and the evidence of those who first witnessed and reported them to others were recorded by a number of scholars. The most authoritative is al-Bukhari. His text is still relied upon today.

The Spread of Islam

After discussing his message secretly with his wife, Khadijah, his cousin Ali, and his friend Abu Bakr, the Prophet decided in the year 622 to leave Mecca, where he had lived in some danger. He migrated to Yathrib (later Madina), whose inhabitants had invited him to come and spread his message. For this reason the history of the Islamic community is considered to have been formally born on the night of the *hejira*, the night of migration, when the Prophet departed Mecca for Madina. The city became the caliphate seat until Damascus replaced it in the year 661. The people of Madina embraced Islam, and gradually, through a series of both military engagements and acts of diplomacy, Muhammad was able to reenter Mecca and to spread the word of Islam throughout the Arabian Peninsula.

The beginning of the *risala*, the message from a transcendental perspective, might be said to have begun with Creation, which is when God ordained things to be. From a temporal perspective, however, it began with the first revelation of the Prophet.

After the death of the Prophet in 632 A.D., his message spread north of the peninsula into Syria, Lebanon, Iraq, Palestine, and Persia. In 638, after the battle of Yarmouk against the Romans, the victorious Arab Muslims entered Palestine. The Romans, during their occupation of Palestine—particularly after their occupation of Jerusalem—had destroyed the Jewish temple and expelled the Jews from Jerusalem in 70 A.D. They had subsequently prevented freedom of religion for Jews and Christians in Palestine until Constantine officially recognized Christianity in the fourth century.

It must be noted that the official church of Byzantium (Eastern Roman Empire), *al-Roum*, was equally oppressive as its pagan forebearers. In particular, it vigorously suppressed the Eastern Christian churches of Syria and the Coptic Church of Egypt. However, since Muslims were by the *Qur'an's* mandate obligated to respect the "People of the Book," their predecessors in receiving divine revelation, they established a covenant with Christians and Jews. Earlier, when the Prophet had migrated to Madina in 622, he had entered into an agreement with the Jewish tribes of Yathrib (later called Madina) when he had journeyed to that city. However, when they joined forces with the Meccans against him, he was forced to turn against them. This brief episode did not harm subsequent Muslim-Jewish relations.

Umar ibn al-Khattab was the second elected *khalifa* or caliph (successor) after the death of the Prophet. He was the head of state of the Muslim nation at the time. About to enter Jerusalem in 638 after his forces had triumphed over the Romans at the Battle of Yarmouk, Umar descended from his horse and called at the gates of the city for all of the leaders of the Christian Church to meet him there. Addressing their elder, Bishop Sophronious, he made the historic Covenant of Umar, requiring all Muslims forever to guarantee Christians freedom of religion, use of their houses of worship, and the right of their followers and pilgrims to visit their holy places. Umar also rescinded the Roman decree banishing Jews from Jerusalem and pledged to protect their freedom of religious practice. The Covenant of Umar was, in effect, the first international guarantee of the protection of religious freedom.

Islam then spread to Egypt in 641 and to all of North Africa by 654. Until the Middle Ages, Islam was present from southern France to China—virtually the entire known world. The spread of Islam was due in part to the military prowess of the Muslim forces. But the message the Muslims were spreading and the manner in which they administered the conquered regions were their strongest asset. They brought with them not only a new and uplifting faith but a system of government which was honest and efficient. They established a civilization that was to flourish for hundreds of years.

By establishing freedom of religion and religious practice for Christians and Jews, they made the followers of these two faiths their principal allies in the countries they sought to enter. In Egypt, for example, it was the Archbishop of the Coptic Church who invited the Muslims to free Egypt from the Roman occupiers in 641. The Coptic Church had been established by St. Mark shortly after the death of Jesus. However, it had been persecuted on religious grounds by the Byzantine Church ever since the Council of Chalcedon had declared monophysitism a heresy in 451. Promises of Coptic support caused Umar ibn al-Khattab to send Amr ibn al-As, the leader of the Muslim forces, into Egypt. With less than 2,000 men, Amr defeated the 12 Roman legions stationed there. The support given the Muslims by the Copts of Egypt insured the success of the campaign.

Although the primary objective of Muslim administration in every new territory was the establishment and propagation of Islam. Muslims also brought to the conquered peoples more effective government administration with a high level of motivation, integrity, and service. Frequently they ended tyrannies that had long existed in many of these countries, liberating rather than subjugating the population.

Throughout the history of Muslim rule, relations between Muslims, Christians, and Jews varied. The Muslims as a rule used leaders drawn from the indigenous population in public administration and did not seek to destroy the local identity of the various areas in which they became implanted. This is why centuries later, notwithstanding the fact that much of the Arab portion of the Islamic nation had been absorbed into the Turkish Ottoman Empire, most of these areas continued to be separate regions with their own institutions, leaders, and particular characteristics. Thus, for example, Egypt and Morocco were entities administered most of the time by their own people. They enjoyed a territorial, administrative, and cultural identity distinct from other regions of Islam. The concept of *Ummah* or nation of Islam never precluded regional and local identity. Islam did not seek to impose radical cultural changes. In fact, because of the flexibility of Islam, it readily became part not only of the belief of the people but of the popular culture.

Islam was also spread by Muslim merchants throughout the known world along the ancient trade routes. People readily converted to a simple religion that appealed to individualism, dignity, logic, and reason. Moreover, it didn't require an organized clergy or the power of a state to propagate or enforce it.

The spread of Islam was halted in France in the year 732 at the battle of Poitiers, but it continued to expand into parts of Asia (e.g., into what is now India, Pakistan, Bangladesh, Afghanistan, parts of the Soviet Union, Malaysia, Indonesia, the Philippines, and China) and into Africa. After the eleventh century, a succession of power struggles among Muslim leaders, as well as regional jealousies and a resurgence of Christian power in the West and in Byzantium, caused the Islamic nation to weaken. The Christian crusades of the eleventh and twelfth centuries battered the Islamic nation, although they were finally brought to an end in 1187 by the famous Muslim general leader of the Ayyubi dynasty of Egypt, Salah al-Din al-Ayyubi. The Ottoman Turkish Empire's expansion was stopped at Vienna in 1683. By the fifteenth century, however, the Arab portion of the Islamic nation had become part of the Ottoman Turkish Empire, which in turn broke apart and was ultimately dismantled by the Western European allies after World War I. Thereafter, the Arab Muslim world fell under the colonial occupation of France and England. Each country in the Arab region obtained its independence from England and France between the years 1922 and 1965, except for Palestine.

A variety of factors brought about the decline of the Islamic state between the twelfth and fifteenth centuries. But the spread of the faith continues even today. The clarity, simplicity, and logic of the faith—as embodied in its tenets and religious practices—are its principal attractions. In addition, the emphasis on individual responsibility and personal commitment as well as the absence of an organized clergy, makes Islam readily transmittable. As the *Qur'an* states Allah is closer to each one than his own jugular vein.

An historical chronology of the Islamic state and its various rulers follows on page 18. It shows the temporal reach and geographic spread of Islamic influence. Islam is a complex political, historical, social, and economic phenomenon; it can be studied and interpreted from a variety of philosophical, historical, and social perspectives. As a faith, however, Islam continues to speak to the modern world irrespective of its other meanings. What constitutes the *Ummah*, the Community of Islam, is not the existence of a political structure but the conscious acceptance of its Muslim participants of Allah's will and their mission on earth.

> ٧٠. وَلَقَدْ كَرَّمْنَا بَنِى آدَمَ وَحَمَلْنَاهُمْ فِى الْبَرِّ وَالْبَحْرِ وَرَزَقْنَاهُم مِّنَ الطَّيِّبَاتِ وَفَضَّلْنَاهُمْ عَلَى كَثِيرٍ مِّمَّنْ خَلَقْنَا تَفْضِيلًا
>
> We have honoured the sons of Adam; provided them with transport on land and sea given them for sustenance things good and pure; and conferred on them special favours, above a great part of Our Creation
>
> Qur'an 17:70

> ١٦. وَلَقَدْ خَلَقْنَا الْإِنسَانَ وَنَعْلَمُ مَا تُوَسْوِسُ بِهِ نَفْسُهُ وَنَحْنُ أَقْرَبُ إِلَيْهِ مِنْ حَبْلِ الْوَرِيدِ
>
> It was We who created man, and We know what dark suggestions his soul makes to him: for We are nearer to him than (his) jugular vein.
>
> Qur'an 50:16

Caravan of camels in the Arabian Desert. (Aramco World Magazine, May/June, 1980; photo by Tor Eigeland.)

Islam in Andalusia

The history of Islam in Spain is the history of one of the most brilliant Islamic civilizations the world has known, the "Golden Caliphate" of the Umayyads. The caliphate was founded by Abd al-Rahman, the sole surviving member of the Umayyad dynasty of Damascus. He had been forced to flee for his life with a younger brother when the Abbasids of Baghdad overthrew the Umayyads as the ruling dynasty in 750. His brother was captured and killed. But, enduring great hardship and peril, Abd al-Rahman—a tall, red-haired, poet warrior—was able to make his way to Spain and Cordoba, the leading city, to claim his rightful position as the surviving head of the Umayyad dynasty.

Islam had come to Spain—or to "Al-Andalus" as it was known to its Moorish rulers—a scant 40 years before when in 710 a raiding party led by a Berber officer, Tariq ibn Malik, crossed the narrow eight mile straight separating Africa from Europe. Less than a year later an invading force of 7,000 men led by Tariq ibn Ziyad landed at Gibraltar (in Arabic *"Jabal Tariq"* or the Mountain of Tariq). And by 718—despite some initial resistance from the Visigoth Christian rulers and their King, Roderick—nearly the whole of the Iberian peninsula was firmly under Muslim control.

So begins the story of the rise of a caliphate that was to become the cultural center of western Islam and seat of learning for Christian Europe. Abd al-Rahman was not able to consolidate his rule for 20 years, since his claim to rule did not go uncontested either in Baghdad or Cordoba. Thus Cordoba's era of splendor really began with his successors, principally Abd al-Rahman II. It was he who imported fashion and culture from the East and set the foundations for the later cultural flowering. He even recruited scholars from the East by offering handsome inducements to overcome their initial reluctance to live in so provincial a city.

By the time of Abd al-Rahman III (912-61), the culture and civilization of Islam in Al-Andalus were in full bloom. Cordoba was a large and vibrant metropolis with a population of roughly 500,000 persons (compared to 40,000 for Paris at the time). There was a university and some 70 libraries containing hundreds of thousands of volumes. Al-Hakim II's library alone contained some 400,000 books, whereas the library of the monastery of St. Gall, had only a few volumes. Science, philosophy, and the arts flourished. The greatest minds in every discipline and from all over Europe and the Levant journeyed to Cordoba to study and learn.

The greatest of these scholars made enduring

contributions to science and letters. Many have become familiar to students in the west under their Latin names, men such as the philosopher Averroes (Ibn Rushd), the mathematicians Arzachel (al-Zarqali) and Alpetragius (al-Bitruji), and the physician Avenzoar (Ibn Zuhr) to name a few.

Perhaps the most notable of all contributions of Muslim scholars to science lay in the field of medicine. Muslim physicians made important additions to the body of knowledge which they inherited from the Greeks. Ibn al-Nafis, for example, discovered the lesser circulation of the blood hundreds of years before Harvey. Al-Zahrawi wrote a masterwork on anatomy and dissection, the *Tasrif,* which was translated into Latin by Gerard of Cremona and became a standard text in European medical schools throughout the Middle Ages. Ibn Baitar wrote a famous work on drugs called ***Collection of Simple Drugs and Food.*** This work served for centuries as an invaluable reference guide to medicinal plants native to Spain and North Africa.

The greatest contribution of Muslim medicine—as it

Far left, The Patio de los Leones in the Alhambra Palace, whose building was begun by Ibn al-Ahmar in 1238 and enlarged by the Nasrid Dynasty, Granada, Spain. (Aramco World Magazine, September/October, 1976; photo by Tor Eigeland.)

Top right, Moorish Golden Tower, Seville, Spain. (Rand McNally.)

Bottom right, detail of the mihrab of the ornate ceiling, Great Mosque, Cordoba, Spain. (Aramco World Magazine, September/October 1976; photo by Tor Eigeland.)

was in other fields—was to distinguish science from pseudo-science. Indeed, in an era of pervasive superstition and ignorance, the great achievement of Islamic scholars was to place the study of medicine and other subjects on a scientific footing. The West didn't achieve a comparable clarity of vision until the Enlightenment. The strongly rationalist orientation of Islamic scholars was especially pronounced in Andalusia, where new scientific developments and fashions coming from the East were often viewed with suspicion. Ibn Hazm, a prominent 11th century Andalusian scholar, put the matter this way. "Those," he said, "who advocate the use of talismans, alchemy, astrology, and other black arts are shameless liars." This pervasively rationalist attitude did much to recommend Islamic science to the rest of the world.

It is a quirk of history that, after periods of exceptional cultural brilliance, periods of decline and decay seem to come most quickly. So it was in Andalusia. With Abd al-Rahman III's successor, the effective but unpopular al-Mansur, the long decline of Muslim rule in Andalusia began. The vibrancy and energy of the culture was sapped by internal strife, as minor Muslim principalities revolted, and by the long and costly effort against the Christian *reconquista*. Muslim religious vigor was periodically renewed by successive Almoravid and Almohad invasions, but the culture was never again to attain the heights it had during the Golden Caliphate.

By 1248 the stronghold in Seville had fallen, and the area of Spain under Muslim control was reduced to the Kingdom of Granada. There, miraculously, Islamic culture survived and prospered for more than two and a half centuries. Ironically, however, it was most likely the Ottoman capture of Constantinople in 1453 that sealed Granada's fate. Soon after, fueled by the Christian fear of Islam, Ferdinand of Aragon and Isabella of Castile—the future patrons of Christopher Columbus—brought the curtain down on one of the most remarkable and glorious civilizations inspired by Islam. The date was January of 1492.

Chronology of major dates in the history of the Islamic State (States)

The following dates are based on the common-era or Christian-era calender.

The Beginning of Islam

622	Hejira, birth of Islam
632	Death of the Prophet Muhammad (born ca. 572)

The Centralized Period

633-661	The four "Righteous Caliphs," seat of khalifa (Caliphate) at Madina
661-750	The Umayyad period, seat of khalifa at Damascus
750-1258	Abbasid period, with seat of khalifa for the first Abbasid period at Baghdad and the second Abbasid period at Samarra

The Empires

1077-1327	The Seljuks
	The Seljuks and the Ottomans extended their control and influence over most of Asia Minor, portions of Central Asia and the Arab world, and into Europe through the Balkans including Albania, Bulgaria, parts of Hungary, Rumania, and Yugoslavia.
1327-1924	The Ottoman or Osmanlu Sultans, later the Ottoman Turkish Empire with capital first at Bursa until 1453, thereafter at Constantinople (Istanbul)
1526-1857	The Moguls
1520-1736	The Safavids

Periods of Regional Rule

I. The Fertile Crescent (Palestine, Syria, Lebanon, Iraq)

638	Conquest of Palestine by Muslims
638-641	Conquest of Syria, Lebanon, and Iraq
641-661	Under the four "Righteous Caliphs" in Madina
661-750	The Umayyad period with capital at Damascus
750-1258	The Abbasid period with capital at Baghdad and Samarra
877-1250	Syria and portions of Lebanon intermittently under Tulunid, Ikhidid, Fatimid, and the Ayyubid dynasties of Egypt

Egypt

641	Conquest of Egypt by Muslims
641-662	Under the control of the four "Righteous Caliphs"
662-868	Under the control of Umayyad and Abbasid Caliphs
868	Beginning of Egyptian-based rulers
868-904	Tulunid dynasty
935-969	Ikhidid dynasty
969-1171	Fatimid dynasty
1168-1250	Ayyubid dynasty
1251-1517	Mamluk dynasty
1517	End of Egypt-based rulers
1517-1805	Under Ottoman Turkish Empire

II. Persia

638	Beginning of conquest
638-640	Completion of conquest
640-661	Under the four "Righteous Caliphs" in Madina
661-820	Under the Umayyad and Abbasid Caliphs
819	Beginning of fragmentation of Persian rulers
819-1055	The Samanid rulers in Northern Persia
820-874	The Tharid rulers in Khorastan
864-1032	The Alid rulers in Tabaristan
868-903	The Sattarid rulers extend throughout most of Persia
879-930	The Seljuk rulers unite Mesopotamia and most of Persia
1037-1194	The Sajid rules in Azerbaijan
	From before the end of the Seljuk rule until 1502, Persia was divided by different rulers in different parts of that region. There were rulers for the areas of Khiva, Azerbaijan, Fars, Luristan, upper Mesopotamia, Diyarbakir, Kerman and Kurdistan.
1502-1736	The Safavid empire
	A portion of the territory now in the Soviet Union was part of Persia, as was a part of Afghanistan.

III. North Africa

669	Muslim conquest on North Africa to Morocco completed
669-800	Under the control of Umayyad and Abbasid Caliphs

789	Beginning of locally-based rulers
789-985	The Idrisid rulers of Morocco
800-909	The Aghlabi rulers of Tunis
900-972	The Fatimids rule over north Africa as part of the Fatimids based in Egypt
972-1148	The Zayri rulers in Tunis
1056-1147	The Al-Moravi rulers of Morocco
1130-1269	The Al-Mohad rulers
1228-1534	The Haisi rulers of Tunis

IV. Afghanistan

711	Conquest of Sindh by Muslims
711-962	Period of uncertainty, fragmented rules, intermittent control by the Umayyad and Abbasid Caliphs and local rulers
962-1186	Ghaznavid rulers
1100-1215	Ghorid rulers
1526-1857	The Mogul Emperors

A portion of this region included territory in what in now the Soviet Union and portions of the Indian sub-continent, in particular part of what is now Pakistan. The Mogul emperors extended their control and influence in certain parts of Russia, Central Asia and the Balkans.

V. Spain

710-712	Conquest of Spain by Muslims
713-750	Under the Umayyad Caliphs
756-1031	Spain-based rulers: The Umayyads of Cordoba, division of Spain and different locally-based rulers, intermittently under the control of the North African rulers
1492	End of Muslim rule in Spain

The Muslim rulers of Spain occupied a portion of southern France for a brief period of time, but no separate rule was established here.

VI. Sicily

827-878	Period of conquest by Aghlabi rulers of Tunis
878-909	Period of uncertainty
909-1071	Under the control of the Fatimids of North Africa and Egypt

The rulers of Sicily occupied southern Italy for close to 300 years, but no separate rule from that of Sicily was established there.

Qarawiyyin Mosque in Fez, Morocco, Almoravid period, built in 859. (Photo by Alex Starkey, London, U.K.)

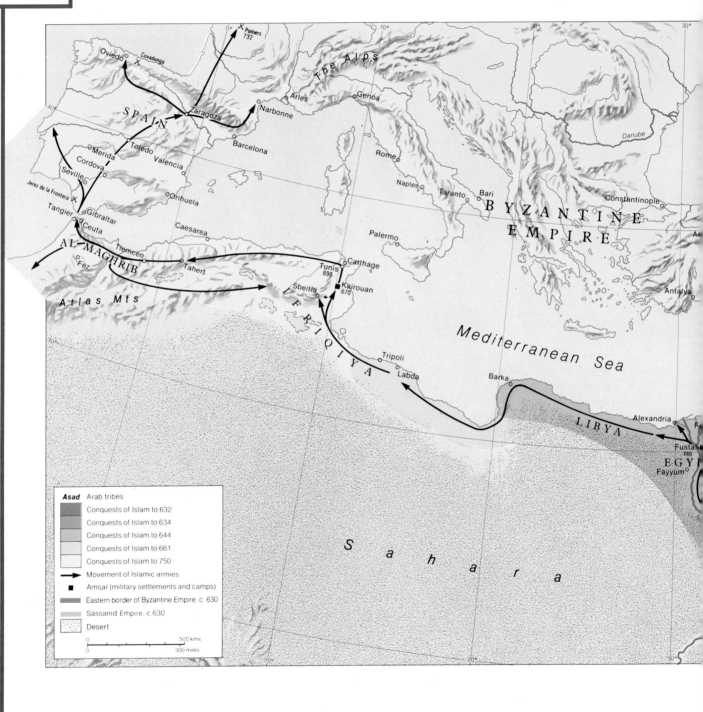

Oviedo
Covadonga
X
SPAIN
Zaragoza
Toledo
Merida
Cordova
Valencia
Seville
Jerez de la Frontera X
Orihuela
Tangier
Gibraltar
Ceuta
Caesarea
AL-MAGHRIB
Tlemcen
Fez
Tahert
Atlas Mts
Sbeitla
IFRIQIYA
Tunis 698
Kairouan 670
Tripoli
Labda
Barka
LIBYA
Alexandria
Fustat 640
EGYPT
Fayyum
Sahara

Portiers 732
The Alps
Arles
Genoa
Narbonne
Barcelona
Rome
Naples
Taranto
Bari
Danube
BYZANTINE EMPIRE
Constantinople
Palermo
Antalya
Mediterranean Sea
Carthage

Asad	Arab tribes
	Conquests of Islam to 632
	Conquests of Islam to 634
	Conquests of Islam to 644
	Conquests of Islam to 661
	Conquests of Islam to 750
→	Movement of Islamic armies
■	Amsar (military settlements and camps)
	Eastern border of Byzantine Empire. c. 630
	Sassanid Empire. c. 630
	Desert

0 — 500 kms
0 — 300 miles

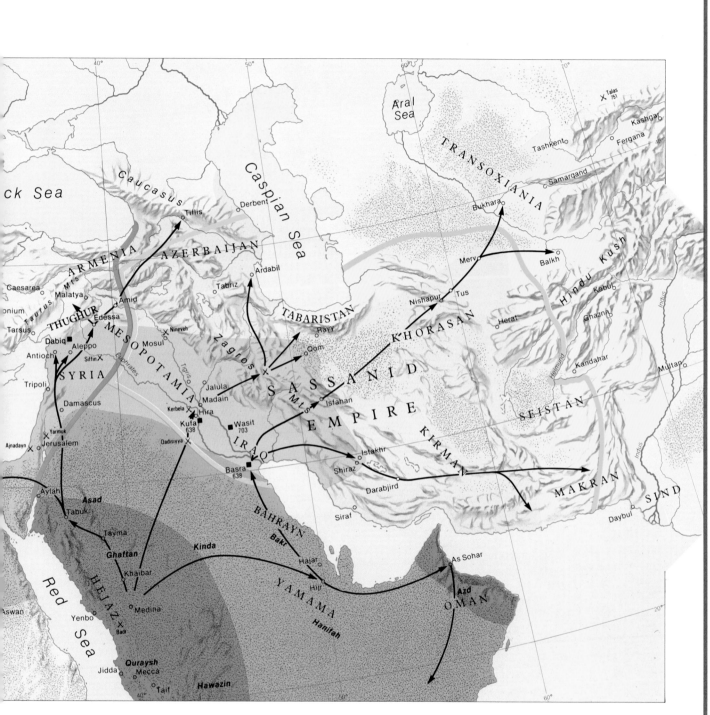

Map showing the conquests of Islam. By the early 700s the Muslims ruled territories stretching over 5000 miles. (Map supplied by Paul Hamlyn Publishing, London, U.K.)

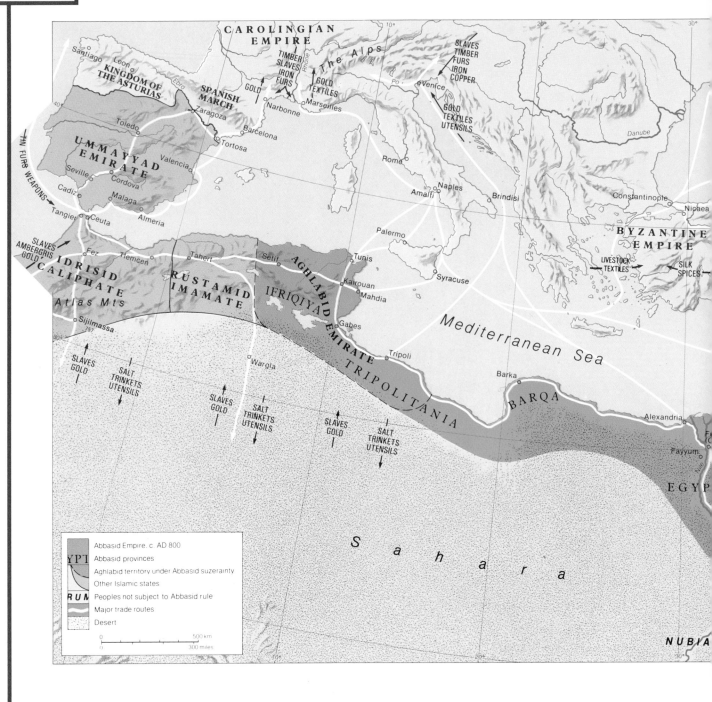

CAROLINGIAN EMPIRE

The Alps

Rhône

Po

SLAVES
TIMBER
FURS
IRON
COPPER

Venice

GOLD
TEXTILES
UTENSILS

Danube

Santiago Leon

KINGDOM OF THE ASTURIAS

SPANISH MARCH

TIMBER
SLAVES
IRON
FURS

GOLD
TEXTILES

Marseilles

Narbonne

Toledo

Zaragoza

UMMAYYAD EMIRATE

Valencia

Barcelona

Tortosa

Rome

Seville Cordova

Naples

Amalfi

Brindisi

Constantinople

Malaga

Cadiz

Almeria

Palermo

Nicaea

Tangier Ceuta

TIN FURS WEAPONS

BYZANTINE EMPIRE

SLAVES
AMBERGRIS
GOLD

Fez Tlemcen

Taheri

Setif

Tunis

IDRISID CALIPHATE

RUSTAMID IMAMATE

AGHLABID EMIRATE

IFRIQIYA

Kairouan

Mahdia

Syracuse

LIVESTOCK
TEXTILES

SILK
SPICES

Atlas Mts

Sijilmassa

Gabes

TRIPOLITANIA

Tripoli

Mediterranean Sea

SLAVES
GOLD

Wargla

Barka

BARQA

SALT
TRINKETS
UTENSILS

Alexandria

SLAVES
GOLD

SALT
TRINKETS
UTENSILS

Fayyum

Nile

SLAVES
GOLD

SALT
TRINKETS
UTENSILS

EGYPT

S a h a r a

YPT

RUM

NUBIA

Legend:
- Abbasid Empire. c. AD 800
- Abbasid provinces
- Aghlabid territory under Abbasid suzerainty
- Other Islamic states
- Peoples not subject to Abbasid rule
- Major trade routes
- Desert

0 — 500 km
0 — 300 miles

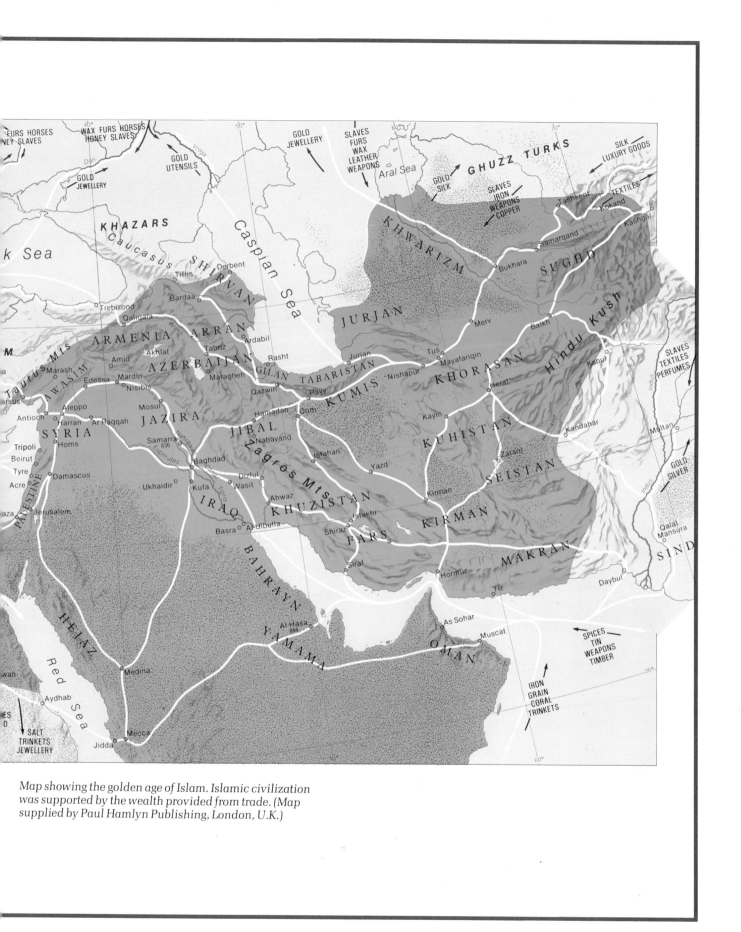

Map showing the golden age of Islam. Islamic civilization
was supported by the wealth provided from trade. (Map
supplied by Paul Hamlyn Publishing, London, U.K.)

Top, Samara Mosque with the spiral minaret, built in the 9th century in Iraq during the Abbasid Period. (Rand McNally.)

Bottom, Suleymaniye Mosque, Istanbul, Turkey built during the Ottoman Period. (Aramco World Magazine, January/February, 1970; photo by Tor Eigeland.)

Panfolov's multi-cultural mosque, Panfolov, Soviet Union. It is on the Soviet side of the frontier with China. The minaret is shaped like a Chinese pagoda. (Aramco World Magazine; photo by Tor Eigeland.)

Registan square, Samarkand, USSR, Timurid Period 14th and 15th centuries. Kusan ibn Abbas, a cousin of the Prophet, brought Islam to Samarkand as early as the 7th century. However, few buildings have remained of the city after the destruction by Chingiz Khan in 1220. (Aramco World Magazine; photo by Tor Eigeland.)

Bottom left, Al-Jawhara Mosque, Lahore, Pakistan. (Rand McNally.)

Top right, Taj Mahal, Agra, India a Tomb-Mosque of Shah Jihan's favourite wife Mumtaz, Mughal Period 1632-54. (Government of India Tourist Office, Chicago.)

The religion of Islam

The Creator has periodically chosen human beings to reveal His messages to humankind. Indeed, the *Qur'an* refers to many Prophets such as Abraham, Noah, David, Isaac, Jacob, Moses, and Jesus. These messages and revelations culminated in Islam and in Muhammed as the last Prophet. The historical evolution and incorporation of prior messages into Islam are clearly stated in the *Qur'an*. Thus Islam is not a new religion. The *Qur'an* refers to Islam as the religion of Abraham, Jacob, Moses, Jesus, and other prophets. It is simply the last of the divine messages to reach humankind through Prophet Muhammad, who was chosen by the Creator as the bearer of his last and all-encompassing revelation. This explains why there exists a strong link between Islam, Christianity, and Judaism. Christians and Jews are referred to in the *Qur'an* as the "People of the Book" because they are the recipients of the messages of the Creator through Moses and the Old Testament prophets and through Jesus, who is believed in Islam to be the fruit of a miracle birth by the Blessed Virgin Mary.

The Qur'an

The *Qur'an* (literally, recitation) contains 114 chapters revealed to the Prophet during a period of 23 years from 609 to 632, the year of his death. The divine revelations were manifested in divine inspiration, which the Prophet sometimes uttered in the presence of his companions. His words were passed on in the oral tradition of his Arabic culture. Some forty years after his death they were transcribed in the written form that has been preserved to date without change. The 114 Suwar (plural of Surah) chapters were revealed to Muhammad in Mecca and Madina. They vary in length. The *Qur'an* is arranged not in the chronological order of its revelation but according to the length of each Surah. The longest is first, and the shortest last. No one throughout the history of Islam has challenged the accuracy of the *Qur'an*.

The Arabian peninsula had a long tradition of literary achievement: Prose and poetry of all types were widely cultivated. The original miracle of the *Qur'an*, however, is its enduring literary achievement. Many

١٣٦- قُوْلُوا امَنَّا بِاللهِ وَ مَا اُنْزِلَ اِلَيْنَا وَ مَآ
اُنْزِلَ اِلَى اِبْرٰهِمَ وَ اِسْمٰعِيْلَ وَ اِسْحٰقَ وَ
يَعْقُوْبَ وَالْاَسْبَاطِ وَ مَآ اُوْتِىَ مُوْسٰى وَ
عِيْسٰى وَ مَآ اُوْتِىَ النَّبِيُّوْنَ مِنْ رَّبِّهِمْ لَا نُفَرِّقُ
بَيْنَ اَحَدٍ مِّنْهُمْ وَ نَحْنُ لَهُ مُسْلِمُوْنَ ◯

Say, Oh Muslims, we believe in Allah and that which is revealed unto Abraham and Isma'il and Isaac and Jacob and the tribes and that which Moses and Jesus received and that which the Prophet received from the Lord. We make no distinction between any of them and unto them we have surrendered. (We are Muslims.)

Qur'an 2:136

١٢٧- وَ اِذْ يَرْفَعُ اِبْرٰهِمُ الْقَوَاعِدَ مِنَ
الْبَيْتِ وَ اِسْمٰعِيْلُ ۚ
رَبَّنَا تَقَبَّلْ مِنَّا ؕ
اِنَّكَ اَنْتَ السَّمِيْعُ الْعَلِيْمُ ◯

And remember Abraham and Isma'il raised the foundations of the House (With this prayer): "Our Lord! Accept (this service) from us: For Thou art the All-Hearing, the All-Knowing.

Qur'an 2:127

Door of the Ka'ba, on the north side, above ground level. Its frame was sent from Istanbul, Turkey in the 17th century. The structure of the Ka'ba is covered with gold leaf embroidered black silk, traditionally given by Egypt as a gift. (Woodfin Camp & Associates; photo by Robert Azzi.)

people refuse to believe that any human being, particularly an illiterate man, could have produced it. Indeed, the belief that the message was revealed by God contributed to the early conversion to Islam of the pagan tribes in the Arabian peninsula. The fact that Prophet Muhammad was a trustworthy person and that his early followers were people whose rectitude was well-established and enduring among the various Arab tribes also contributed to early conversions.

The *Qur'an* is written in such a way that it evokes profound emotions in the reader. The analogies, maxims, and stories provide imagery of great "psychological moment," full of an *elan* which imparts an uplifting sense of great destiny in life and lasting fulfillment in heaven. The richness of its form and content invites constant rereading. Moral values are intertwined with history, and the details of daily life are placed on a continuum with life in the hereafter. Its topics range from the most specific to the most general and include the past and future, life on earth, and existence of the soul after death. Its topics cover all aspects of human interaction as well as relations between man and his Creator. It is, in short, a comprehensive and integrated guide to life.

The Three Fundamental Unities of Islam: God, Humankind, and Religion

Islam is a universal faith for all times, all places, and all peoples. It is predicated on the belief that there is but one God, *Allah*, the Creator of the universe and of humankind. The *Qur'an* opens with the words, "In the name of Allah, the Merciful, the Compassionate." Mercy and compassion are His principal qualities. The relationship which exists between God and His creation is based on one religion. These fundamental unities are the foundation of faith.

The *Qur'an* refers to the creation of the earth and other celestial bodies out of the darkness of chaos. Scientific theories that have evolved about the creation highlight the unity of the universe. If God created this unique universe and shaped humankind to inhabit it, it follows that God would also have communicated with humankind through a single religion, even though it be in successive revelations. Islam is the last and most all-encompassing message of God.

If one believes that there is but one humankind which is part of a single universe created by one God, then one believes in an interrelationship among all created things. Religion in this context is a set of rules that regulate the relationship between the Creator and the created and establish the basis of accountability in the hereafter. It also sets forth the framework for permissible economic, social and political systems and formulates the principles and rules through which people should deal with one another. In effect, it provides a variety of prescriptions and guidelines as well as inspiration.

In this respect, Islam is very much a law-oriented religion. It provides the guidelines and principles upon which laws and regulations can be established. The influence of Islam must not be viewed in a narrowly legalistic light but rather as providing a framework which guarantees basic fairness and justice to all.

Islam is holistic, requiring that its followers have *iman* (faith) to fulfill the requirements of its religious tenets. The Muslim is required to express his *Ibada*, service to *Allah*, through his deeds, conduct, and words. The *Qur'an* enjoins that Muslims do good and abjure evil. Life in this world is a passage, and the eternal soul shall be judged by the Almighty on Judgment Day by intentions as well as by deeds. Reward and punishment shall be meted out in heaven and hell, but *Allah* is merciful to those who repent and do good. Repentence and mercy are among Islam's great themes.

Bearing Witness to the One and Only God (shehada)

Allah in Arabic implies the one and only true God, the beginning and the end of everything, neither born nor giving birth. The *Qur'an* states that He is beyond human description, but is referred to in the *Qur'an* by ninety-nine attributes, such as the merciful, the compassionate, the forgiving. Together with the command to bear witness and acknowledge the singularity, centrality, unity, and uniqueness of God, the believer is enjoined to confess that Muhammad is God's messenger and prophet.

Religious Tax (zakat)

Although required by the *Qur'an*, *zakat* is specified in detail only in the practice and teachings of the Prophet and in later interpretations. It is the payment of a certain percentage of one's income to support the needy and to fulfill other objectives of the community. While this can be roughly equated to a combination of taxation and charity, *zakat* is different from *sadaqa*, charity, which is equally mandated by the *Qur'an* but left to the discretion of the individual Muslim, depending upon circumstances. *Sadaqa* is both tangible and intangible—a kind word, for example, may be a form of *Sadaqa*. But *Zakat* is tangible. It is paid at the end of the Ramadan fast. Non-Muslims, the people of the book (Christians and Jews), are not required to pay *Zakat* but another tax, called *Jizyah*.

Fasting during Ramadan (siyam)

Fasting from dawn to sunset during the month of *Ramadan*, the ninth month in the Islamic lunar calendar, is required of those whose health permits. (The Islamic lunar calendar is 11 days shorter than the Gregorian calendar, thus the annual shift of Ramadan's occurrence in relationship to the Gregorian calendar.) It is a complete fast, requiring that nothing be taken into the body but needed medication. During *Ramadan* there is an emphasis on piety and religious observances. Those who are ill or traveling do not have to fast during Ramadan but must compensate by fasting and by contributing to the *Zakat*.

The Pilgrimage (hajj)

The pilgrimage to Mecca once in one's lifetime is required of all those who have the physical and financial ability to make the journey. The practice derives from the divine mandate given Muhammad to rebuild

بَاۤ اَيُّهَا الَّذِيْنَ اٰمَنُوْا كُتِبَ عَلَيْكُمُ الصِّيَامُ

كَمَا كُتِبَ عَلَى الَّذِيْنَ مِنْ قَبْلِكُمْ

لَعَلَّكُمْ تَتَّقُوْنَ

Ye who believe! Fasting is prescribed to you as it was prescribed to those before you, That ye may (learn) self-restraint,...

Qur'an 2:183

Mosque of the Haram, Mecca, Saudi Arabia. It was converted into a mosque by the Prophet in the year 630. The building consists of a vast colonnade surrounding a courtyard in the center of which is the Ka'ba. The Ka'ba is a cube-shaped structure measuring 13m x 11m x 16m. It is believed that the Ka'ba was built by Abraham the Patriarch. In the northeast corner is the Black Stone, an object of reverence. Within the courtyard there is the burial place of Abraham and the Zamzam well. The mosque was enlarged in the 7th century. It underwent additions in the 8th, 9th, 16th, and 20th centuries. The government of Saudi Arabia has significantly improved its interior in the last decade. (Woodfin Camp & Associates; photo by Robert Azzi.)

"Islam has been built on five (pillars) testifying that there is no god but Allah and that Muhammad is the Messenger of Allah, performing the prayers, paying the zakat, making the pilgrimage to the House, and fasting in Ramadan."
The Prophet's Hadith.

the first temple of worship to God in Mecca. The pilgrimage requirement makes this desert city a gathering place for people from all parts of the world once a year. The rituals of the *hajj* were established by the Prophet. They emphasize repentance, resulting in forgiveness by God. The practice also strengthens the bond among the faithful from all walks of life and regions of the world. It is performed during the Islamic lunar month of *Dhu al-hijja*.

Prayers (salat)

The *Qur'an* does not state the number and manner of prayers; these were established by the Prophet. The required individual prayers are said five times a day: at dawn, noon (when the sun is at the center of the sky), afternoon (when the sun is halfway to sunset) sunset, and night (after sunset but before sunrise). The only required communal prayer is the Friday noon prayer. Like the Christians' Sunday or the Jews' Sabbath, Muslims consider Friday the last day of Creation.

Prayers can also be communal; that is, in fact, the preferred way. When so conducted, the prayers are led by an *imam*, who is usually either a person schooled in Islam or simply one among the group who is more knowledgeable, older, or recognized by the others as being especially pious.

Muslims stand shoulder to shoulder and kneel a number of times, depending on whether it is the morning prayer (twice) or the late-night prayer (four times). Standing shoulder to shoulder, irrespective of status in life, symbolizes equality before God. In Islam, as the Prophet said, no man is better than another save for his piety, which only *Allah* can judge. At each kneeling, the Muslim places his forehead on the ground, a symbol of the equality of all men, humility, worship of the Creator, and the fact that from earth we come and to

earth we return. All praying Muslims face Mecca, where the *Ka'ba* is located. It is the *qibla* (the direction) which provides unity and uniformity for all Muslims. At an earlier time, it was the practice to face Jerusalem, the second holiest city in Islam. The *Ka'ba* holds the remnants of Abraham's temple.

The *imam* does not necessarily have any special religious status in *Sunni* tradition just because he is the prayer leader. However, he could be a person whose schooling or training conferred on him special status, as is the case with the *ulema* (or scholars, plural of *alem*). One attains this status after having pursued an extensive education in theology throughout secondary, college, and graduate study at a theological university.

Before prayers, Muslims are required to perform ablutions, which include washing the face, arms, and feet in a ritual prescribed by the Prophet. This is not only for the purposes of cleanliness, but to provide a break from prior activity. Before ablutions and prayers, a Muslim must confirm within himself his intention to pray.

The prayers are usually announced by means of a summons or call to prayer (the *adhan*) by the *muadhin*, who chants or intones it. There is no particular religious status conveyed by this responsibility; the *muadhin* is usually a pious member of the community who has a particularly strong or resonant voice. The call to prayer starts with *"Allahu akbar"* (God is great), words frequently used by Muslims either in prayers or in other contexts as a reaffirmation of the oneness and omnipotence of the Creator. The expression *"al-hamdu lillah"* (thanks be to God) is also among the phrases most commonly used by Muslims. They are used in any situation in which a grateful or thankful response is apposite. They are a reminder that God's will and bounty are everything.

The mosque is a symbol of the uncompromising

A muadhin intones the call to prayer. The first call to prayer from the top of the Ka'ba was made by Bilal a black Ethiopian freed slave who embraced Islam. He was chosen by the Prophet for his reputed meladious and carrying voice. (Aramco World Magazine, November/December 1985; photo by John Feeny.)

nature of Islamic monotheism. It has a distinctive architecture, which includes a minaret for the call to prayer. It does not contain any images that might be associated with religious idolatry, which Islam forbids. The architecture of mosques built over fourteen centuries in various parts of the Muslim world is an unsurpassed artistic legacy. The floors of mosque are sometimes covered with straw mats or rugs. Muslims remove their shoes before entering so as not to soil the place where they touch their foreheads to the floor to pray.

٢٥٦ لَا إِكْرَاهَ فِى الدِّينِ قَد تَّبَيَّنَ الرُّشْدُ مِنَ الْغَيِّ فَمَن يَكْفُرْ بِالطَّاغُوتِ وَيُؤْمِنْ بِاللَّهِ فَقَدِ اسْتَمْسَكَ بِالْعُرْوَةِ الْوُثْقَىٰ لَا انفِصَامَ لَهَا وَاللَّهُ سَمِيعٌ عَلِيمٌ

Let there be no compulsion in religion: Truth stands out clear from Error: whoever rejects evil and believes in God hath grasped the most trustworthy hand-hold, that never breaks. And God heareth and knoweth all things.

Qur'an 2:256

"The best of you are those who have the most excellent morals."
The Prophet's Hadith.

Mosque of Umar, also known as Dome of the Rock Mosque, Umayyaad Period, 690-2. It is the third shrine of Islam after the Ka'ba in Mecca and the Prophet's Mosque in Madina. The building covers a naked rock representing the summit of Mount Moriah, from which the Prophet ascended to heaven. Umar Ibn al-Khattab, the second caliph entered Jerusalem on foot, in 638 after defeating the Romans at the battle of Yarmouk, to symbolize his respect for this holy city. Before entering the city he gathered the Christian religious leaders to assure them that henceforth freedom of religion would be preserved for the People of the Book. Ever since religious denominations have always been in control of their own sites and monuments. Bishop Sophrinuous the eldest of Christian clergy is reported to have offered Umar ibn al-Khattab to pray inside the Church of the Holy Sepulchre. However, he refused and responded: "I fear that if I should pray inside the church that Muslims will claim it later for their own use." Instead he went to pray on the barren rock upon which the mosque was built. This mosque is a symbol of Muslim respect for Christianity and peaceful coexistence of the three monotheistic faiths. (Aramco World Magazine, July/August 1974; photo by William Tracy.)

Islamic Law— the Sharia

And nor shall we be punishing until we had sent them an Apostle.

وَمَا كُنَّا مُعَذِّبِينَ حَتّى نَبْعَثَ رَسُولًا ۝

Qur'an 17:15

The *Qur'an* is the principal source of Islamic law, the *Sharia*. It contains the rules by which the Muslim world is governed (or should govern itself) and forms the basis for relations between man and God, between individuals, whether Muslim or non-Muslim, as well as between man and things which are part of creation. The *Sharia* contains the rules by which a Muslim society is organized and governed, and it provides the means to resolve conflicts among individuals and between the individual and the state.

There is no dispute among Muslims that the *Qur'an* is the basis of the *Sharia* and that its specific provisions are to be scrupulously observed. The *Hadith* and *Sunna* are complementary sources to the *Qur'an* and consist of the sayings of the Prophet and accounts of his deeds. The *Sunna* helps to explain the *Qur'an*, but it may not be interpreted or applied in any way which is inconsistent with the *Qur'an*.

Though there are other sources of law—i.e., *ijma'*, (consensus), *qiyas*, (analogy), *ijtihad*, (progressive reasoning by analogy)—the *Qur'an* is the first and foremost source, followed by the *Hadith* and *Sunna*. Other sources of law and rules of interpretation of the *Qur'an* and the *Hadith* and *Sunna* follow in accordance with a generally accepted jurisprudential scheme.

The *Qur'an* contains a variety of law-making provisions and legal proscriptions interspersed throughout its chapters (*suwar*) and verses (*ayat*). A number of rules exist for interpreting these provisions, such as the position of a given *ayah* within the context of the *surah*, which in turn is interpreted in accordance with its place in the sequence of revelations, its reference to other revelations, and its historical context in relation to particular conditions which existed at the time of the given revelation. These and other rules are known as the science of interpretation (*ilm usul al-fiqh*). According to these rules, for example, one initially is to refer to a specific provision and then to a general provision dealing with a particular situation. No general provision can be interpreted so as to contradict a specific provision, and a specific rule will supersede a general proposition. A general provision, however, is always interpreted in the broadest manner, while a specific provision is interpreted in the narrowest manner. Reasoning by analogy is permitted, as are applications by

"Avoid condemning the Muslim to *Hudud* whenever you can, and when you can find a way out for the Muslim then release him for it. If the Imam errs it is better that he errs in favor of innocence (pardon) than in favor of guilt (punishment)."
The Prophet's Hadith.

"Were people to be given in accordance with their claim, men would claim the fortunes and lives of (other) people, but the onus of proof is on the claimant and the taking of an oath is incumbent upon him who denies."
The Prophet's Hadith.

Al-Azhar Mosque showing the inner courtyard, founded by the Fatimid Dynasty in 970-972. It is the oldest university in the world and the most influential source of Islamic learning. Its graduates are among the religious leaders of all Muslim societies. (Aramco World Magazine, September/October 1973; photo by John Feeney.)

analogy, except where expressly prohibited. Simplicity and clear language are always preferred. Similarly, the clear spirit of certain prescriptions cannot be altered by inconsistent interpretations. A policy-oriented interpretation within the confines of the rules of jurisprudence is permissible and even recommended, as is the case with the doctrine of *ijtihad* (progressive reasoning by analogy).

Muslim scholars do not consider Islam to be an

٥٨-إِنَّ اللهَ يَأْمُرُكُمْ أَنْ تُؤَدُّوا الْأَمَٰنَٰتِ
إِلَىٰ أَهْلِهَا وَإِذَا حَكَمْتُمْ
بَيْنَ النَّاسِ
أَن تَحْكُمُوا بِالْعَدْلِ
إِنَّ اللهَ نِعِمَّا يَعِظُكُم بِهِ
إِنَّ اللهَ كَانَ سَمِيعًا بَصِيرًا

Lo! Allah commandeth you that ye restore deposits to their owners, and, if ye judge between mankind, that ye judge justly. Lo! comely is this which Allah admonisheth you. Lo! Allah is ever Hearer, Seer.
Qur'an 4:58

evolving religion, but rather a religion and legal system which applies to all times. It is, therefore, the application that is susceptible to evolution. Indeed, the provisions of the *Qur'an* are such that by their disciplined interpretation, with the aid of the *Hadith* and *Sunna* and other sources of interpretation, Islam can, as intended, provide the solution to contemporary social problems.

Fourteen centuries ago Islam was a spiritual, social, and legal revolution. Its potential for effecting progress remains unchanged. This is essentially the belief of enlightened fundamentalist Muslims. Islamic fundamentalism is not, therefore, a regressive view of history and contemporary reality. Islam at the height of its civilization, between the seventh and eleventh centuries, was neither repressive nor regressive. It was a progressive, humanistic, and legalistic force for reform and justice.

Schools of thought in Islam

Islamic jurisprudence has developed over fourteen centuries. Over that span of time, various schools of jurisprudence have emerged, each with its own interpretation and application of the *Sharia*. Many schools splintered farther, creating schools following different interpretive approaches and applications.

The flourishing abundance of ideas and views attests to the intellectual depth and breadth of Islamic jurisprudence. However, nothing precludes a given state from codifying the *Sharia* so as to provide for more certainty of the law and clarity and consistency in its application. Many Muslim states have done so, the most advanced being Egypt, where the presence of the thousand-year-old Al-Azhar University (originally devoted solely to Islamic studies but now to all disciplines) and centuries of legal tradition have converged to make Islamic law a source of inspiration for the entire Muslim world.

The Sunni and the Shia

The *Sunni* tradition, which today comprises approximately 85-90 percent of all Muslims, differs from *Shia* tradition, which comprises the remainder of the Muslim world. The distinction between the two traditions essentially derives from different approaches to governance. The *Sunni* believe, based on specific provisions of the *Qur'an* and the *Sunna*, that the Muslim people are to be governed by consensus (*ijma'*) through an elected head of state, the *khalifa*, according to democratic principles. The Shia, however, believe that the leader of Islam, whom they refer to as the *imam* rather than the *khalifa*, must be a descendant of the Prophet. The concept is the basis for a hereditary hierarchy in the *Shia* tradition.

The *Shia* movement dates from the period when a group of Muslims wanted Ali ibn abu Talib, the cousin and son-in-law of the Prophet, to become the *khalifa* instead of Abu Bakr, who had been elected the first khalifa following the death of Muhammad in 632. They advanced his candidacy on the basis of heredity. However, they were out voted. Ali ultimately became the fourth *khalifa*, succeeding Uthman, who succeeded Umar, who succeeded Abu Bakr. But Ali was over-

The Green Dome of the Prophet's Mosque in Madina, Saudi Arabia. (The Embassy of Saudi Arabia, Information Office, Washington, D.C.)

Inset, Courtyard of the Mosque of the Prophet in Madina, Saudi Arabia, founded by the Prophet in 622. It is the second holy shrine of Islam after the Ka'ba in Mecca. The Prophet layed out this rectangular mosque next to his house. The mosque was enlarged and redecorated by the Abbasids, the Mamluks, and the Ottomans throughout the years. After he died, the Prophet was buried there. (The Embassy of Saudi Arabia, Washington, D.C.)

thrown by the rebellion of Muawia, the governor of Syria, whose seat was in Damascus. Muawia rebelled against Ali because he attributed the assassination of his kinsman Uthman to Ali's followers. Ali was subsequently assassinated after losing the *Tahkim* (arbitration) to Muawia. His followers then constituted what would today be called a political party to reinstate him

O ye who believe! Be steadfast witness for Allah in equity, and let not hatred of any people seduce you that ye deal non justly. Deal justly, that is nearer to your duty. Observe your duty to Allah. Lo! Allah is informed of what we do.

Qur'an 5:8

٩ - يَا أَيُّهَا الَّذِينَ آمَنُوا كُونُوا قَوَّامِينَ لِلَّهِ شُهَدَاءَ بِالْقِسْطِ وَلَا يَجْرِمَنَّكُمْ شَنَآنُ قَوْمٍ عَلَى أَلَّا تَعْدِلُوا اعْدِلُوا هُوَ أَقْرَبُ لِلتَّقْوَى وَاتَّقُوا اللَّهَ إِنَّ اللَّهَ خَبِيرٌ بِمَا تَعْمَلُونَ ○

And hold fast, All together, by the rope which God (stretches out for you), and be not divided among yourselves; and remember with gratitude God's favour on you; For ye were enemies and He joined your hearts in love, so that by His grace, Ye became brethren; And ye were on the brink of the pit of fire, and He saved you from it. Thus doth God make His signs clear to you: that ye may be guided.

Qur'an 3:103

١٠٣ - وَاعْتَصِمُوا بِحَبْلِ اللَّهِ جَمِيعًا وَلَا تَفَرَّقُوا وَاذْكُرُوا نِعْمَتَ اللَّهِ عَلَيْكُمْ إِذْ كُنْتُمْ أَعْدَاءً فَأَلَّفَ بَيْنَ قُلُوبِكُمْ فَأَصْبَحْتُمْ بِنِعْمَتِهِ إِخْوَانًا وَكُنْتُمْ عَلَى شَفَا حُفْرَةٍ مِنَ النَّارِ فَأَنْقَذَكُمْ مِنْهَا كَذَلِكَ يُبَيِّنُ اللَّهُ لَكُمْ آيَاتِهِ لَعَلَّكُمْ تَهْتَدُونَ ○

and to secure succession to the *Khalifa*.

In 680 Hussain, one of Ali's sons, led a number of Muslims who were then rebelling against the ruling *khalifa* to try to establish in the area between Iran and Iraq a caliphate based on heredity from the Prophet. However, Hussain was lured into Iraq, and there at a place called Karbala he and his followers were massa-cred. Hussain's martyrdom spurred the *Shia* movement in Iraq and Iran. The anniversary of Karbala is commemorated every year by the *Shia* population. In Iran, in particular, it is conducted by means of a large popular demonstration in which people publicly weep and flagellate themselves as a sign of their remorse.

Top, Shrine of Fatima, sister of the Eighth Imam Ali ar-Rida, at Qum, Iran. The Shia believe that the only legitimate successors of Muhammad are the descendants of his cousin and son-in-law Ali. Their shrines and those related to them are great places of pilgrimage for the Shias. (Roger Wood Library, Deal Kent, England.)

Bottom, Map showing the distribution of the Shia from 1500 to 1980; prepared by Dr. Shafiq Ismail.

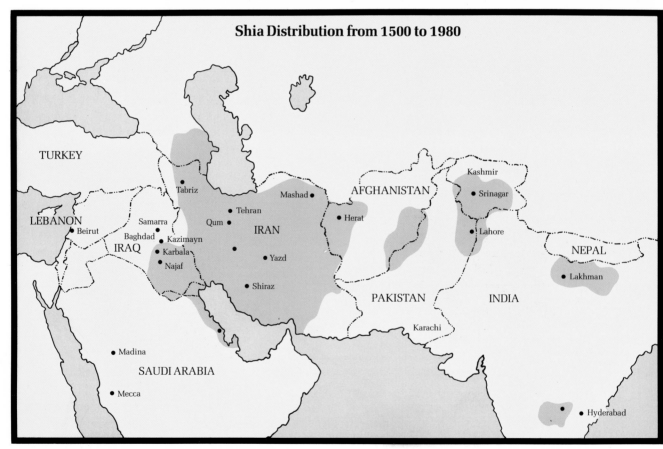

Shia Distribution from 1500 to 1980

TURKEY

LEBANON

Beirut

Tabriz

Samarra

Baghdad

Kazimayn

Karbala

Najaf

IRAQ

Qum

Tehran

IRAN

Yazd

Shiraz

Mashad

Herat

AFGHANISTAN

Kashmir

Srinagar

Lahore

NEPAL

Lakhman

PAKISTAN

INDIA

Karachi

Madina

SAUDI ARABIA

Mecca

Hyderabad

The political rift between followers of the principle of election and those favoring descent from the Prophet generated some other differences between *Sunni* and *Shia* approaches to jurisprudence. For example, the *Shia* view the sayings of Fatima, the daughter of the Prophet, and his cousin Ali (Fatima's husband), the fourth *khalifa* of the Islam, as equally authoritative as the *Sunna* of the Prophet. The *Sunni* do not. There are other differences involving the structure of Islam, such as existence of an organized *Shia* clergy, which does not exist in the *Sunni* tradition. Among them the *Shia* allow the *imam* much wider latitude in government than the *Sunni* ever could in light of the principles of consensus and equality. The most important of all differences between *Sunni* and *Shia* relates to the interpretation of the *Qur'an*. The *Sunni* look more to the letter of the *Qur'an*; the *Shia* look more to its spirit. In Arabic the distinction is referred to as *al-dhaher* (the apparent) versus *al-baten* (the hidden) meaning of the *Qur'an*. Thus the *Shia* religious hierarchy plays a determining role in interpreting the *Qur'an*. This role reinforces their spiritual and temporal influence in *Shia* society.

Sunni Jurisprudence

The *Sunni* follow any one of four major schools on jurisprudence founded by *imams* ibn Hanbal, abu Hanifa, Malek, and el-Shafei, scholars of the ninth to eleventh centuries. These schools, referred to respectively as the *Hanbali*, *Hanafi*, *Maliki*, and *Shafei*, are followed by different Muslim states either entirely or in part. Egypt is traditionally *Maliki*. Saudi Arabia is traditionally *Hanbali*, although the country follows more closely the teachings of *imam* Muhammad Abdal-Wahab, a *Hanbali* reformer of the early 1800's. Even though there are differences in interpretation of the *Sharia* among these authorities, they are all recognized as valid.

In its most glorious period, from the seventh to the thirteenth centuries, Islam produced a legal system founded on scientific knowledge and nurtured by a faith that has endured the test of time. But during that period it was *ijtihad* (progressive reasoning by analogy) which produced the most far-reaching developments. Reformers like ibn Taymiyah (late 1200's) was one of many great jurist-philosophers who opened new horizons in the knowledge and understanding of Islam's application to the needs of society. But in the twelfth century, *ijtihad* was pronounced ended by some theologians of the time. They argued that all was to be known was known. Consequently, Islamic jurisprudence became somewhat stagnant until its contemporary resurgence under the aegis of Al-Azhar scholars and other modern reformers of the last two centuries, such as al-Ghazali, al-Afghani, and Muhammad Abdu. Contemporary jurisprudential developments continue the work begun in past ages, meeting individual requirements and collective demands for resolving the problems and conflicts of modern life, while remaining compatible with Islam.

Sufism

The **Sufi** movement is a mystical strain in Islam which reflects the need of individuals to transcend formal religious practices in order to attain higher levels of spiritual fulfillment. The Sufis are represented in all schools of thought in Islam and found in all Muslim communities. Because of its mystical, spiritual character, Sufism appeals more to individuals and small groups. It does not constitute either a sect or a school of thought, but is rather a spiritual or transcendental practice which persists despite criticism from orthodox theologians. Sufis believe they follow the Prophet's mysticism, particularly during the Meccan period of the revelations. Thus, in their practices there is much meditation and solitary or group recitation of prayers and incantations of their own religious formulas. They seek a life of ascetic pietism, shunning worldly pleasures and seeking the inward purity of a relationship with God through love, patience, forgiveness, and other higher spiritual qualities.

Their influence on the development of Islam is more significant than is usually recognized. Their ascetic piety and rigidly ethical conception of Islamic society have influenced generations of Muslims. They have also had from time to time strong political influence. What characterizes Sufis the most is their "inwardism" or belief that the *Sharia* only regulates external conduct, whereas inward feelings are matter strictly between each person and the Creator. Because of their emphasis on the love of God, they have developed the doctrine of *Tawakul* (reliance on God), which is central to the relationship between Man and God. Sufism also has had a significant impact on the practical aspects of administering a state.

Illumination showing a scene of the life of Jalal al-Din al-Rumi, the greatest mystic poet of Islam. After he became a Sufi, he invented the whirling dance of his sufi order. It is reported that upon hearing the hammering rythm of goldsmiths he began to move in ectasy to that rythm. In the picture one of his followers rushes to embrace his feet. Orthodox Sunni frown on Sufism. (Bodleian Library, Oxford, England.)

The social system and morality of Islam

An important *Hadith* (saying) of the Prophet is that religion is not what one formally or ritualistically practices but how one deals with others. It is therefore not sufficient to be pious without performing deeds which demonstrate one's beliefs. It is reported that the Prophet once entered a mosque and saw at prayer a venerable old man with a long white beard. He was told that the man was in the mosque all day long, worshipping and dispensing the words of Allah to others. The Prophet then asked how he earned his living and was told that a merchant, not known for his piety, supported him. The Prophet remarked that of the two, the merchant was indeed the more worthy.

Every Muslim is the recipient, guardian, and executor of God's will on earth; his responsibilities are all encompassing. A Muslims's duty to act in defense of what is right is as much part of his faith as is his duty to oppose wrong. The Prophet once said, "If someone among you sees wrong he must right it by his hand if he can (deed, conduct, action). If he cannot, then by his tongue (speak up, verbally oppose); if he cannot, then by his gaze (silent expression of disapproval); and if he cannot, then in his heart. The last is the minimum expression of his conviction (faith, courage)."

Living the faith is *ibada*, service to God through service to humankind.

The preservation of a social order depends on each and every member of that society freely adhering to the same moral principles and practices. Islam, founded on individual and collective morality and responsibility, introduced a social revolution in the context in which it was first revealed. Collective morality is expressed in the *Qur'an* in such terms as equality, justice, fairness, brotherhood, mercy, compassion, solidarity, and freedom of choice. Leaders are responsible for the application of these principles and are accountable to God and man for their administration. It is reported that a man went to Umar, the second *khalifa*, to talk to him. It was nighttime, and a candle burned on Umar's desk. Umar asked the man if what he wanted to discuss was personal. The man said that it was, and Umar extinguished the candle so as not burn public funds for a private purpose. Leaders in Islam, whether heads of state or heads of family or private enterprise, have a

Top, Students of Islam in a Madrassah (school). Traditionally the madrassah was attached to the mosque. (Aramco World Magazine, September/October 1973; photo by John Feeney).

٩٢- لَن تَنَالُوا الْبِرَّ حَتَّى تُنفِقُوا مِمَّا تُحِبُّونَ ۚ وَمَا تُنفِقُوا مِن شَيْءٍ فَإِنَّ اللَّهَ بِهِ عَلِيمٌ ۝

By no means shall ye attain righteousness unless ye give (freely) of that which ye love; and whatever ye give, of a truth God knoweth it well.

Qur'an 3:92

And to be firm and patient, in pain (or suffering) and adversity, And throughout all periods of panic. Such are the people of truth, the God-fearing.

Qur'an 2:177

وَالصَّابِرِينَ فِي الْبَأْسَاءِ وَالضَّرَّاءِ وَحِينَ الْبَأْسِ ۗ أُولَٰئِكَ الَّذِينَ صَدَقُوا ۖ وَأُولَٰئِكَ هُمُ الْمُتَّقُونَ ۝

"Whosoever of you sees an evil action, let him change it with his hand; and if he is not able to do so, then with his tongue; and if he is not able to do so, then with his heart-and that is the weakest of faith."
The Prophet's Hadith.

Saudis at Computer Terminals. (Embassy of Saudi Arabia, Information Office, Washington, D.C.)

higher burden or responsibility than others.

There is a relation in Islam between individual responsibility and the rights and privileges derived from membership in the community. Individual obligations must be met before one can claim a portion from the community of which he is part. Each member of a society must fulfill his own obligations and rely on others to fulfill theirs before that society can acquire the necessary reservoir of social rights and privileges which can then be shared by all. The notions of brotherhood and solidarity not only impose upon the community the duty to care for its members, but also require each person to use his initiative to carry out individual and social responsibilities according to his ability.

Equality

The equality of all Muslims is emphasized repeatedly throughout the *Qur'an*. It is because of that concept that Islam under the *Sunni* tradition does not have an ordained clergy. There is a direct relationship between every man and his Creator, and there can be no intermediary. This particular closeness between the individual and God is paramount in belief as well as in practice.

It is frequently argued that Islam is not a religion that provides for full equity among Muslims. Indeed, because Islam makes distinctions between men and women; not all rights and privileges available to men are available to women. For example, a male Muslim inherits twice the share of the female, but then a male relative has the financial responsibility to care for a needy female relative. Also, a male Muslim has the right to unilaterally divorce his wife, while she can only divorce her husband through a judge's determination. Custody of children from a divorce is given the mother, boys till age 9 and girls till age 12. Thereafter custody reverts to the father, provided that he is fit. However, the fact that there is not absolute parity in all rights and privileges does not mean that women do not share an overall equality with men. It must also be noted that certain social practices in some Muslim countries are not required by Islam, but have simply evolved in the course of time as a result of indigenous cultural factors.

Islam differentiates between Muslims and non-Muslims and between the "People of the Book" (*dhimmi*) and others. Only Muslims have the right to elect the *khalifa*. In judicial matters the oath of the Muslim prevails over that of the non-Muslim. There are therefore some differences between males and females in Islam,

between Muslims and *Dhimmis,* and Muslims and non-*Dhimmis.*

Individual Responsibility

The search for justice is one of the continuing quests of humankind. It is the quest that is prescribed by the *Qur'an* for every Muslim. Social and individual justice are evolving concepts which depend largely upon a variety of external considerations. Above all, Islam seeks to inculcate within every Muslim the need to seek justice and to apply it to himself as well as to others. Because Muslims believe that God is the beginning and the end of everything, all is preordained by *Qadar* (divine will). *Qadar* does not imply inaction, but, rather, acceptance. It requires the strength to change what can be changed and the fortitude to accept what cannot.

Individual responsibility is a cornerstone of Islam. Every Muslim is accountable to his Creator for what he himself does or fails to do—as well as for others for whom he may be accountable—and for things that he has control over. As in Western legal codes, individual responsibility is predicated on the intent and motive of the actor in light of his ability to do good and to avoid evil or harm to others. Thus Islam believes in free will, and to the extent that this exists a person is responsible for its exercise in the framework of Islamic morality. But the relativity of human justice is not to be confused with the absoluteness of divine justice whose application every Muslim expects without fail on judgment day. Because of the Muslim's belief in accountability in the hereafter, his oath is valid evidence in any judicial or extra-judicial process.

Forbearance and Forgiveness

A Muslim is accountable for what he does and what he fails to do in accordance with not only the letter but also the spirit of the law. However, even though Islam imposes a number of very rigid requirements and appears formalistic and inflexible, one of the basic premises of the relationship among Muslims, and between Muslims and others, is derived from one of the basic premises of the relationship between a Muslim and his Creator, namely, forbearance and forgiveness.

In one of the Prophet's *Hadiths* it is stated that a person could do such evil during his lifetime that there might be between him and the doors to hell only one step and then he could repent and ask for God's forgiveness and do one good deed and enter heaven. By the same token, a person may during his life do so much

Interior of the Prophet's Mosque in Madina. (Aramco photo).

٣٦- وَاعْبُدُوا اللّهَ وَلَا تُشْرِكُوا بِهِ شَيْئًا
وَبِالْوَالِدَيْنِ إِحْسَانًا
وَبِذِى الْقُرْبَى وَالْيَتَامَى وَالْمَسَاكِينِ
وَالْجَارِ ذِى الْقُرْبَى وَالْجَارِ الْجُنُبِ
وَالصَّاحِبِ بِالْجَنْبِ وَابْنِ السَّبِيلِ
وَمَا مَلَكَتْ أَيْمَانُكُمْ
إِنَّ اللّهَ لَا يُحِبُّ مَنْ كَانَ مُخْتَالًا فَخُورًا

Serve God, and join not any
partners with Him; and do good—
To parents, kinsfolk, orphans,
those in need, neighbours who
are near, neighbours who are
strangers; the companion by
your side, the way-farer (ye
meet), and what your right
hands possess: For God loveth
not the arrogant, the
vainglorious;—

Qur'an 4:36

"Actions are but by intention and
every man shall have but that
which he intended."
The Prophet's Hadith.

"None of you (truly) believes
until he wishes for his brother
what he wishes for himself."
The Prophet's Hadith.

good as to be one step removed from heaven and then
do one evil deed that would be sufficient to earn him
hell. The meaning of the *Hadith* is to emphasize that,
even though a person may do good throughout his life,
he should never be absolutely certain that the good he
has done all along is sufficient to carry him through; he
should not forget that one bad deed could overcome all
the good ones. Conversely, a person who has done evil
all his life may repent even at the last moment and with
one good deed earn paradise.

The element of forbearance and forgiveness has to be
predicated on knowledge, awareness, and truth. Forbearance and forgiveness depend on the believer's rec-
ognition and acceptance of what he has done and his
genuine repentance with an intent not to repeat the

misdeed. That is why Muslims are encouraged to for-
give the bad deeds of others committed against them.

Allah is described in the *Qur'an* as the Forgiving
and the Merciful. Everything is forgivable by Allah
except *Shirk* (the negation of the existence of the
Singularity, Uniqueness and Oneness of the Creator.)
Even so the mercy of God is infinite. A man was once
brought to the Prophet for trial because he denied the
existence of God. Upon review of the facts, it appeared
that the man was in despair over a personal tragedy. He
had been found in the desert throwing his spear to the
sky and screaming that he wanted to kill God for the
injustice that he had suffered. The Prophet replied, "Is
it not enough that he acknowledged the existence of
God to want to kill him?" The man was set free.

Women in Islam

As in most of the nomadic tribes of the ancient world, women were deemed unimportant in pre-Islamic Arabia. Indeed, in a society shaped by the rigors of desert life, women were relegated to the margins of community life.

The advent of Islam fundamentally altered the status of women in several ways. First, and most importantly, it overturned tradition by according women equal status before Allah. No longer were women denied a human face. Their souls like the souls of men were precious to Allah. They, like men, were worthy of dignity and respect. As a result of this new status—and the revolution it worked on Arab society—women became pillars of early Muslim society and were counted among its strongest supporters. Several women—notably Fatimah, daughter of the Prophet Muhammad and wife of Ali, the fourth caliph—even played important roles in the propagation of the faith. To the Shia, for example; Fatimah is an authoritative source of the Prophet's sayings and deeds.

The status of women under Islam also altered as a consequence of the spread of the religion itself. As Islam became a world religion and its influence spread the character of Arab society changed, requiring that women take a larger role in society. As men hurriedly left their flocks and businesses to fight for Islam, women readily assumed the burdens and responsibilities of the home.

The Prophet set an example for the treatment of women in marriage through his relationship with his first wife Khadijah. Although fifteen years his elder, Muhammad remained a faithful and devoted husband for twenty-six years, contrary to the tradition of polygamy which prevailed at the time in Arabia. After her death Muhammad remarried, but he always remembered Khadijah with love and spoke of her with reverence. Khadijah was, in fact, Muhammad's first convert to Islam and his strongest supporter in the struggle to establish the new faith.

Aishah bint abu Bakr (613-678) was Muhammad's favorite wife of later years. Noted for her education and intelligence, in particular her ability to read and write, she was often consulted about the teachings of the Prophet after his death. She played an important role in the life of the early community, most famously by opposing the succession of Ali after the death of Uthman, the third khalifa.

The new, elevated status of women is apparent in numerous *Qur'anic* proscriptions which set out women's rights and obligations. On protecting the dignity and self-respect of women, for example, the *Qur'an* is

Indonesian Muslim girls in modern traditional Islamic dress. (Aramco World Magazine, May/June 1988; photo by Nik Wheeler).

Behold! the angels said: "O Mary! God giveth thee glad tidings of a word from Him: his name will be Christ Jesus, the son of Mary, held in honour in this world and the hereafter and of (the company of) those nearest to God;...

٤٥- إِذْ قَالَتِ الْمَلَائِكَةُ يَمَرْيَمُ إِنَّ اللَّهَ يُبَشِّرُكِ بِكَلِمَةٍ مِنْهُ ۚ اسْمُهُ الْمَسِيحُ عِيسَى ابْنُ مَرْيَمَ وَجِيهًا فِى الدُّنْيَا وَالْآخِرَةِ وَمِنَ الْمُقَرَّبِينَ ۞

Qur'an 3:45

O Mankind: Be careful of your duty to your Lord who created you from a single soul and from it created its mate and from them twain hath spread abroad a multitude of men and women. Be careful of your duty toward Allah in whom ye claim (your rights) of one another.

Qur'an 4:1

ا۔ يَا أَيُّهَا النَّاسُ اتَّقُوْا رَبَّكُمُ
الَّذِيْ خَلَقَكُمْ مِّنْ نَفْسٍ وَّاحِدَةٍ
وَّخَلَقَ مِنْهَا زَوْجَهَا وَبَثَّ مِنْهُمَا
رِجَالًا كَثِيْرًا وَّنِسَاءً ۚ
وَاتَّقُوا اللهَ الَّذِيْ تَسَاءَلُوْنَ بِهٖ
وَالْأَرْحَامَ ۚ
إِنَّ اللهَ كَانَ عَلَيْكُمْ رَقِيْبًا ○

"Jahimah came to the Prophet, said, 'O Messenger of Allah! I intended that I should enlist in the fighting force and I have come to consult thee.' He said: 'Hast thou a mother?' He said, 'Yes.' He said: 'Then stick to her, for paradise is beneath her two feet.'"
The Prophet's Hadith.

O Mankind! Lo! We have created you male and female and have made you nations and tribes that ye may know one another. Lo! The noblest of you in the sight of Allah is the best in conduct.

Qur'an 49:13

۱۳۔ يَا أَيُّهَا النَّاسُ إِنَّا خَلَقْنَاكُمْ
مِنْ ذَكَرٍ وَّ أُنْثَى
وَجَعَلْنَاكُمْ شُعُوْبًا
وَّقَبَائِلَ لِتَعَارَفُوْا ۚ
إِنَّ أَكْرَمَكُمْ
عِنْدَ اللهِ أَتْقَاكُمْ ۚ
إِنَّ اللهَ عَلِيْمٌ خَبِيْرٌ ○

"The most perfect of the believers in faith is the best of them in moral excellence, and the best of you are the kindest of you to their wives."
The Prophet's Hadith.

Kuwaiti woman studying in a library. (Embassy of Kuwait, Washington, D.C.)

45

emphatic and unequivocal: One of the seven *hudud* crimes is maligning a woman's reputation.

The *Qur'an,* of course, acknowledges and makes provision for differences between men and women. Indeed, on these differences is erected an elaborate structure of individual and social rights and obligations. Some appear inequitable on the surface but on examination reveal a deeper logic and reasonableness. A man, for example, stands to inherit twice as much as a woman, but then he must provide for his own wife and family and relatives should the need arise.

The same holds true of traditional rules of dress and behavior. Women are enjoined to cover their bodies (except for the face and hands) and lower their gaze in the presence of men not related to them. Moreover, although women and men are subject to the same religious obligations—such as prayer, fasting, pilgrimage to Mecca—women pray separately from men. Nonetheless, these rules of dress and behavior—however restrictive they may appear to Western eyes—serve a social function. In societies which by tradition provide few protections outside the family, they insure a woman's integrity and dignity. For that reason, too, men are enjoined to lower their eyes before women and to be appropriately covered from above the chest to the knees.

In other areas, women enjoy a strict parity with men. A woman's right to own property is just as absolute as a man's. Male kin cannot handle a woman's financial interests without her permission. A woman must specifically consent to marriage and cannot be forced to accept a husband she does not approve of. In cases of divorce—in a prominent departure from traditional practice—women have exclusive guardianship rights over children up to early puberty. Although a husband has the right to divorce his wife unilaterally—a right not shared by women—a wife can divorce her husband on specific legal grounds by court order.

In education, too, women have the same rights as men. In contemporary Muslim society, in fact, women have attained the same levels of education as men and in many countries occupy positions of power and influence.

Nothing in Islam prevents a woman from accomplishing herself or attaining her goals. Societies may erect barriers, but nothing in the spirit of the *Qur'an* subjugates women to men. In time, of course, social barriers will disappear—as they are disappearing now—because Muslim women will expect and demand it. As a result, it can only be expected that women will play an increasingly larger role in Islamic society and surpass the contributions of early Muslim women.

The parties should either hold Together on equitable terms, Or separate with kindness

فَإِمْسَاكٌ بِمَعْرُوفٍ أَوْ تَسْرِيحٌ بِإِحْسَانٍ

Qur'an 2:229

Lo! Allah enjoineth (orders) justice (or injustice) and kindness (or unkindness) and to give to (one's) kinsfolk…

٩٠۔ إِنَّ اللَّهَ يَأْمُرُ بِالْعَدْلِ وَالْإِحْسَانِ وَإِيتَاءِ ذِي الْقُرْبَى وَيَنْهَى عَنِ الْفَحْشَاءِ وَالْمُنْكَرِ وَالْبَغْيِ يَعِظُكُمْ لَعَلَّكُمْ تَذَكَّرُونَ

Qur'an 16:90

"What did the Prophet do when in his house? She said, 'He served his wife,' meaning that he did work for his wife." The Prophet's Hadith.

Young Muslim students in Guyana. (Aramco World Magazine, November/December 1987; photo by Larry Luxner).

The Islamic Calendar

The Islamic calendar is unique among the major calendars of the world. Unlike the Gregorian calendar and others based on the astronomical solar year—the length of time it takes for the earth to revolve around the sun—the Islamic calendar is based on the lunar year.

The lunar calendar is comprised of 12 lunar months like the calendar based on the solar year. However, since each month begins and ends with the new moon—a period lasting 29 days, 12 hours, 44 minutes, and 2.8 seconds—each lunar year contains only 354 days (or 355 on leap years) as opposed to 365 and ¼ days for the astronomical year. There are 11 leap years in every cycle of 30 years, the intercalated day always being added to the last day of Dhu al-Hijjah, the last month of the year.

As a consequence of the fewer number of days in the lunar year, the lunar calendar is unrelated to the progression of the seasons. The month of Rajab, for example, could occur in summer in one year and the middle of winter 15 years later. Relative to the solar year, the lunar calendar progresses by 10 or 11 days each year so that 33 Muslim years are approximately equal to 32 Gregorian years.

The difference in the length of the lunar year accounts for some of the difficulty in converting dates from the Islamic (*Hijri* or "Hijrah") system to the Gregorian and vice versa. The following equation can be used to calculate the Hijrah year in which the corresponding Gregorian year began:

$$A.D. = 622 + (32/33 \times A.H.)$$

The Islamic calendar was devised in the seventh century in response to the exigencies of governing the far-flung Abbasid empire. It also was created, not incidentally, to glorify the triumph of the new religion. Other calendars in use at the time were tied to other states and religions, and so, the historian al-Biruni tells us, the caliph Umar ibn al-Khattab decided to develop a new calendar based on the advent of Islam, taking July 16, 622 A.D., the date of the Hijrah or the Prophet's sojourn from Mecca to Madina, as the starting point of the calendar of the Muslim era.

The Muslim months are:

Muharram	Jumada al-Awwal	Ramadan
Safar	Jumada al-Thani	Shawwal
Rabi' al-Awwal	Rajab	Dhu al-Qi'dah
Rabi' al-Thani	Sha'ban	Dhu al-Hijjah

Page from a Qur'an printed in Istanbul, Turkey in 1387 A.H. Surah (chapter) 112:1-4: This surah is the cornerstone of Muslim's belief in the unity, centrality, and uniqueness of Allah.

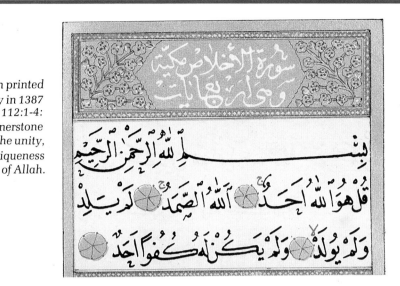

Say: He is God, The One and Only; God, the Eternal, Absolute; He begetteth not, nor is He begotten; and there is no likeness to Him.

Qur'an 112:1-4

Astrolabe used by early astronomers, 14th century. (Rand McNally).

The following holidays are observed among Muslim communities throughout the world:
'Id al-Fitr, also known as the Little Feast, marks the end of the great fast of Ramadan. It occurs on the first day of the month of Shawwal.
'Id al-Adha, the Feast of Sacrifice, also known as the Great Feast, falls seventy days after 'Id al-Fitr, on the 10th of the month of Dhu al-Hijjah.
Ra's al-Sannah, New Year's Festival, falls on the first of the month of Muharram.
Mawlid an-Nabi, the Prophet's Birthday, is celebrated on the 12th day of the month of Rabi' al-Awwal.
Lailat al-Isra' wa al-Mi'raj, this festival commemorates the Prophet's miraculous journey, from Mecca to Jerusalem to heaven and then back to Mecca in the same night, is celebrated on the 27th day of the month of Rajab.

Economic aspects of Islam

The *Sharia* contains prescriptions, proscriptions, recommendations, suggestions, general principles, and guidelines that may be considered the basis for an overall economic theory. It is important to remember, however, that such a theory must be part of the holistic vision of Islam and the integration of all aspects of human endeavor and interaction.

In one *Hadith*, the Prophet said that one should work in life as if one were going to live forever. This saying does not mean that there should be no sense of immediacy or urgency to action. Rather it suggests that there should be continuity in life. It also suggests that one should not be obsessed with attaining immediate results and worldly success. On the other hand, the *Hadith* goes on to state that one should act with respect to life in the hereafter as if one were to die tomorrow. In this, it conveys a sense of urgency about having one's conscience in good order. These correlative maxims rest on the ethical-moral prescription in the *Qur'an* to do good and abjure evil.

While there exist numerous economic theories consistent with the *Qur'an*, the ethical-moral basis of all of them must be the same. Because Islam is a way of life as well as a form of government, a social structure as well as a regulatory norm for interpersonal relationships, business is not something different and apart from all these other aspects of social life. It is a part of human life like any other. Islamic society preserves the notions of free enterprise and social solidarity, social responsibility and humanistic concern for all. It precedes self-interest, though that also is the object of many specific guarantees.

The Prophet, in another *Hadith*, once said that nine-tenths of all *rizk* (the bounty of God, which includes income) is derived from commerce. That, to a large extent, explains the drive of Muslims over the centuries to meet their economic needs through commerce, industry, agriculture and various forms of free enterprise. Profits are very much a part of such activities, provided they are lawfully obtained (*halal*). However, profits cannot overshadow the duties of brotherhood, solidarity, charity and they are, of course, subject to *zakat*.

Top, dhow, the traditional Gulf boat, sailing away. (Aramco World Magazine; photo by Tor Eigeland).

Bottom, oil Tankers in the Persian Gulf. (Embassy of Kuwait, Washington, D.C.)

Top, scene from King Abd Al Aziz airport in Jeddah. (International Airport Project . Information Office, Embassy of Saudi Arabia, Washington, D.C.)

Bottom, aerial view of the Mosque of Salah al-Din al-Ayyubi in Damascus, Syria. (Embassy of Syria, Washington, D.C.)

١٧٧- لَيْسَ الْبِرَّ اَنْ تُوَلُّوْا وُجُوْهَكُمْ
قِبَلَ الْمَشْرِقِ وَالْمَغْرِبِ
وَلٰكِنَّ الْبِرَّ مَنْ اٰمَنَ بِاللّٰهِ
وَالْيَوْمِ الْاٰخِرِ وَالْمَلٰئِكَةِ وَالْكِتٰبِ
وَالنَّبِيّٖنَ
وَاٰتَى الْمَالَ عَلٰى حُبِّهٖ ذَوِى الْقُرْبٰى
وَالْيَتٰمٰى وَالْمَسٰكِيْنَ
وَابْنَ السَّبِيْلِ وَالسَّآئِلِيْنَ وَفِى الرِّقَابِ
وَاَقَامَ الصَّلٰوةَ وَاٰتَى الزَّكٰوةَ
وَالْمُوْفُوْنَ بِعَهْدِهِمْ اِذَا عَاهَدُوْا

It is not righteousness that ye turn your faces towards east or west; but it is righteousness—To believe in God and the Last Day, and the Angels, and the Book, and the Messengers; to spend of your substance, out of love for Him, for your kin, for orphans, for the needy, for the wayfarer, for those who ask, and for the ransom of slaves to be steadfast in prayer, and practice regular charity; to fulfill the contracts which ye have made;

Qur'an 2:177

51

Legitimacy of Profit

Islam distinguishes between legitimate (*halal*) and illegitimate (*haram*) profit, of which usury (*riba*) is a part. To a large extent, the problem of defining usury has arisen over matters dealing with the practices of financial institutions in the West, namely the payment of interest which in the traditional Islamic view is considered a form of *riba*. By collecting a predetermined, fixed interest, the Muslim neither earns a profit from his work nor shares in risk of his capital. Speculation is prohibited, as is undue profiting from the need or misery of others. Nothing, however, proscribes income derived from what would be equivalent to mutual fund or special trust earnings or other contemporary forms of financing investments where the investor also bears the burden of potential loss. In fact, there exists in Islamic law a form of contract called *muqaradah*. Here a person entrusts capital to another person for commercial investment. The risk-taking elements justifies the profits, which are neither fixed nor predetermined.

The ethical-moral foundation of all economic relations is based on the distinction between *halal* and *haram* as set forth in the *Sharia*. The particular context of a given action, considering the interests of the community and the rights of all individuals involved, determines whether it may be deemed *halal* or *haram*. Although this may appear to be vague to the non-Muslim, it is nonetheless sufficiently clear to the Muslim because of his belief in the omniscience of God.

Fulfillment of Obligations

In all of his dealings, the Muslim is required to pay his debts as well as due compensation to those who work for him. He is to honor his obligations and stand by his word. Rectitude in business dealings and personal relations is as important to the Muslim as is any other tenet of faith. Religion must be lived. Thus ethics, morality, and religion are inseparable. That is why Muslims frequently do business by means of oral agreements or a handshake as opposed to a written contract. This also explains why there is usually a reluctance to adjudicate claims on an adversarial basis, where artful arguments may be found to rationalize or justify changing positions. Therefore, in cases of disagreement in business practices, Muslims frequently resort to arbitration. The practice is no different from that which has developed in non-Muslim societies: Each side selects an arbitrator who in turn selects a third person. It is common for both sides to agree on the arbitrator, usually a person whose faith, piety, and reputation for fairness is well-established in the community.

Because of the role of the individual in Islam as the recipient and bearer of God's will on earth, the sense of individual dignity, pride, and honor is very marked in the Muslim. Ideally, position in life and economic status should not be distinguishing factors in Islam, though in modern societies these distinctions have developed. Respect for the individual applies to form as well as substance and extends to all aspects of human interaction. A Muslim's word is still his bond, and his dignity is his most cherished attribute. An appeal to higher values is more convincing than an appeal to practicality and pragmatism. Human relations are more important than practical considerations. Loyalty and fidelity are among the most highly regarded qualities. Rectitude is expected, and undue advantage is considered base. Fairness is both a means and an end, irrespective of the practical realities. Honesty is not a virtue but an expected trait in every Muslim. In today's world of business these values have eroded.

Role of Work

In Islam, work, intellectual as well as physical, is considered the basis of all richness and property. There is both a right to work and a right to the product of that work, as well as a right to benefit from the rewards of divine providence. Work must always have an ethical-moral component, either in itself or in its outcome (i.e., charity, contributing to the community, etc.). There is in the philosophical sense no intrinsic wealth, although the right of inheritance is protected and specifically prescribed under *Sharia*, which allows for the preservation of property, its devolution and accumulation. Nonetheless, there is the implied premise that wealth should be legitimized through work. In addition, wealth must also be used for good of others, such as the needy, and for the community as a whole. The greater one's wealth and power, the greater is the responsibility to use them properly. In many respects work is considered a form of piety.

Economic freedom extends to work, property, and the choice of how to use one's capabilities and resources. The individual has the freedom to choose the type of work he does, and he has the right to work in an environment that does not impinge upon his personal dignity. Only in freedom can an individual choose how to use the fruits of his labor, that is, to use his wealth for personal aggrandizement or for the benefit of the community. There is a prohibition against *jah*, the flaunting of one's achievement in the face of others, particularly the less fortunate. This reflects the values of equality and humility symbolically manifested in the five daily prayers, when people stand side by side,

O ye who believe do not eat up your property among yourselves in wrong. But there be amongst you trade in mutual good will.

يَا أَيُّهَا الَّذِينَ آمَنُوا لَا تَأْكُلُوا أَمْوَالَكُمْ بَيْنَكُمْ بِالْبَاطِلِ إِلَّا أَنْ تَكُونَ تِجَارَةً عَنْ تَرَاضٍ مِنْكُمْ

Qur'an 4:29

"The buyer and the seller have the option (of cancelling the contract) as long as they have not separated, then if they both speak the truth and make manifest, their transaction shall be blessed, and if they conceal and tell lies, the blessing of their transaction shall be obliterated."
The Prophet's Hadith.

"The truthful, honest merchant is with the prophets and the truthful ones and the martyrs."
The Prophet's Hadith.

"Whoever cultivates land which is not the property of any one has a better title to it."
The Prophet's Hadith.

Great Mosque of Damascus, courtyard with mosaics showing square tower. Umayyad period 705 to 715. It includes the tomb of Saint John the Baptist. (Angelo Hornak, London, England).

Turkish seal dating from 1318. (City Lord, Jerusalem).

shoulder to shoulder, kneeling in unison and putting their foreheads to the ground.

Property

The *Sharia* recognizes the right to private property and its uses (provided it is *halal*), save for the right of the community to "eminent domain." The use of property in accordance with the best interests and dictates of the owner is safeguarded, provided the rights of others are protected. There is throughout the notion that the utilization of wealth must balance the rights of the owner against the rights and interests of the community, which extends to the preservation of the property itself. Use is permissible; abuse and destruction are forbidden.

Property of whatever sort is not considered merely the personal privilege of the one who owns it. Ownership brings with it a certain responsibility towards the property itself, its use and benefits. The relationship between man and his Creator and the social responsi-

bilities of a Muslim require that property be used not only for one's personal advantage and benefit but also for the advantage and benefit of the community. This does not mean that every commercial, industrial, or agricultural enterprise must ultimately turn into a charitable activity, but there must be human, ethical, and moral factors that relate to the use of property. Thus, if the choice is between an ethical-moral consideration and profit, the former prevails over the latter, other things being equal.

Contracts

Because every Muslim is accountable before both *Allah* and his community, a great deal of faith is placed in a Muslim's word. Contractual freedom is required and implies the ability to make free choices without undue influence. The attempt to control certain segments of the market or certain phases of a given mechanism that may either control prices or affect the natural laws of a free economy is considered *haram*. Thus

Islamic economic liberty is inherently similar to the notion of free enterprise and socially responsible capitalism. The principles of Islamic economic theory would invalidate transactions in which deceit or undue influence is used by one person against another.

Contracts of various types are regulated by the *Sharia* and are subject to the concepts of *halal* and *haram*. Contracts are essentially predicated on the free will of the parties and must manifest the true expression of their intent. Economic activities based on implied contracts are also balanced by a variety of what would now be called equitable principles to insure against undue influence and lack of fairness, which affect questions of competence, validity, rescission, and damages. Thus the theory of market observation (*hisba*) postulates that there is a notion of accountability for the market and responsibility for its supervision. The theory originally applied to the traditional agricultural markets and their related commercial markets in the period from the seventh to the twelfth century. It can be compared to market and control mechanisms such as the Federal Reserve Board's control of currency or the Securities and Exchange Commission's control of stock transactions.

Individual contracts, implied contracts, and contracts of adhesion are to be regulated in such a way as to enhance fairness, produce equity, protect the weak and the unwary, and promote social interests. The logical extension of these principles is that no one can enrich himself to the detriment of others. In such a case the injured party has a right to compensation for his loss, not to exceed the extent of profit of the one causing the unjust loss. All of these notions of equity, including protection of the public (consumers, users, etc.), have now emerged in the legal systems of the modern world.

Modern Legal Systems

All Muslim states have legal systems with courts, laws and judges, like elsewhere in the world. There are, however, differences among Muslim states. In some countries, such as Egypt, Jordan, Lebanon, Morocco, Syria and Tunisia, there is a tradition of legal codification and jurisprudence. Structures for the administration of justice are also well-developed. There is a three-level judiciary comprising trial courts, appellate courts, and a supreme court. The practice of adjudication of claims with representation by counsel is well-established. In some countries, such as Saudi Arabia, Kuwait, the United Arab Emirates and other Gulf states, there is less of a tradition of codification and a greater reliance on the *Sharia*. But there are also in these countries a number of laws applying to contracts, commercial relations, agency and the like, in addition to a judicial system and a jurisprudence specific to commercial matters. In the last decade, moreover, many countries have enacted civil and commercial codes—Algeria, Kuwait, and the United Arab Emirates, for example—which are mostly modeled after the Egyptian Civil Code of 1948. The Egyptian code was taken in turn from the French Civil Code and adapted to the *Sharia*. In the 1980's, Pakistan and the Sudan, which have codified legal systems, have been in the process of changing their laws to conform to the *Sharia*.

Silver pendant. Muslim jewelry is noted for its intricate details and fine craftsmanship. (Aramco World Magazine, March/April 1979; photo by Ian Yeomans).

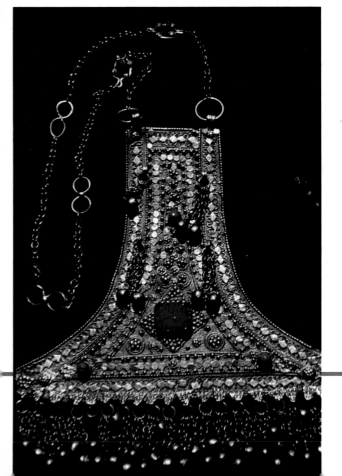

And O my people! give just measure and weight, nor withhold from the people the things that are their due: Commit not evil in the land with intent to do mischief.

Qur'an 11:85

It is We who have placed you with authority on earth, and provided you therein with means for the fulfillment of your life: Small are the thanks that ye give!

Qur'an 7:10

Islamic Civilization

An Overview

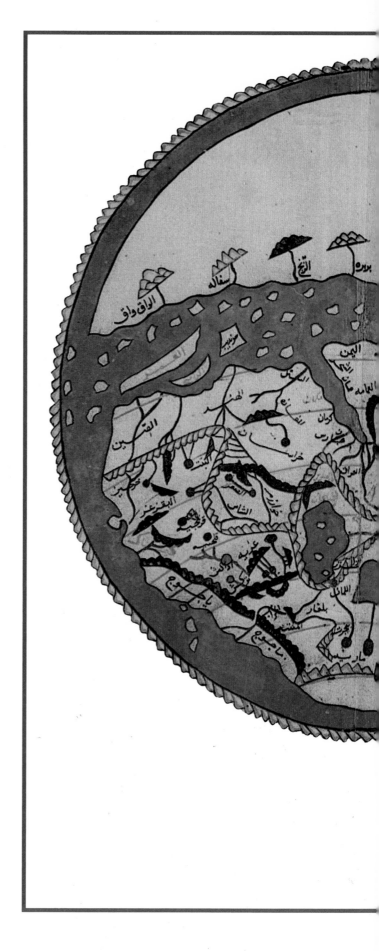

Because Islam originated and has developed in an Arab culture, other cultures which have adopted Islam have tended to be influenced by Arab customs. Thus Arab Muslim societies and other Muslims have cultural affinities, though every society has preserved its distinguishing characteristics. Islamic culture inherited an Arab culture born in the desert, simple but by no means simplistic. It has an oral tradition based on the transmission of culture through poetry and narrative. However, it has been the written record that has had the greatest impact on civilization. Islam civilization is based on the value of education, which both the *Qur'an* and the Prophet stressed.

Knowledge and Education

In the Pre-Islamic period, one of the traditions was that of the *mu'allaquat* (literally "the hangings"). In the city of Mecca, poets and writers would hang their writings on a certain wall in the city so that others could read about the virtues of their respective tribes. Their travels from city to city and tribe to tribe were the means by which news, legends, and exploits would become known. The tradition continued as the *Qur'an* was first memorized and transmitted by word of mouth and then recorded for following generations. This popular expression of the Arab Muslim peoples became an indelible part of Islamic culture. Even today Muslims quote the *Qur'an* as a way of expressing their views and refer to certain maxims and popular tales to make a point.

Great centers of religious learning were also centers of knowledge and scientific development. Such formal centers began during the *Abbasid* period (750-1258 A.D.) when thousands of mosque schools were established. In the tenth century Baghdad had some 300 schools. Alexandria in the fourteenth century had 12,000 students. It was in the tenth century that the formal concept of the *Madrassah* (school) was developed in Baghdad. The *Madrassah* had a curriculum and full-time and part-time teachers, many of whom were women. Rich and poor alike received free education. From there *Maktabat* (libraries) were developed and foreign books acquired. The two most famous are *Bait*

Map of the known world by al-Idrisi circa 1154. Al-Idrisi was a poet, a student of medicine, and an avid traveler. He is known best as a geographer and historian. (Rand McNally).

١١٤- فَتَعَلَى اللهُ الْمَلِكُ الْحَقُّ ۚ وَلَا تَعْجَلْ بِالْقُرْآنِ مِن قَبْلِ أَن يُقْضَى إِلَيْكَ وَحْيُهُ ۖ وَقُل رَّبِّ زِدْنِي عِلْمًا ۗ

Then exalted be Allah the True King! And hasten not (O Muhammad) with the Qur'an ere its revelation hath been perfected unto thee, and say: My Lord! Increase me in knowledge.

Qur'an 20:114

Ceramic Bowl decorated with calligraphy. (*Aramco World Magazine, May/June 1976; photo by Peter Keen).*

Page from a book in Arabic, called "Collection of Simple Drugs and Food," written in the 10th century by the Andalusian botanist Ibn Baitar. It is a collection of medicinal plants. (Bodleian Library, Oxford, England).

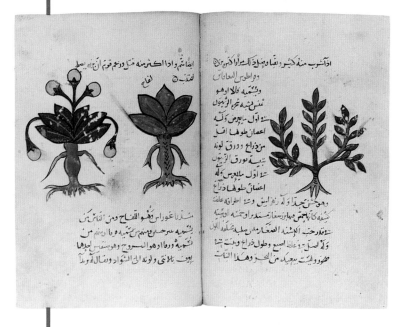

al-Hikmah in Baghdad (ca. 820) and Dar al-Ilm in Cairo (ca. 998). Universities such as Al-Azhar (969 A.D.) were also established long before those in Europe.

Islamic history and culture can be traced through the written records: Pre-Islamic, early Islamic, *Umayyad*, the first and second *Abbasid*, the Hispano-Arabic, the Persian and the modern periods. The various influences of these different periods can be readily perceived, as can traces of the Greek, the Indian, and the Pre-Islamic Persian cultures. Throughout the first four centuries of Islam, one does not witness the synthesis or homogenization of different cultures but rather their transmittal through, and at times their absorption into, the Islamic framework of values. Islam has been a conduit for Western civilization of cultural forms which might otherwise have died out. Pre-Islamic poetry and prose, which was transmitted orally, was recorded mostly during the *Umayyad* period (661-750 A.D.)

when the Arab way of life began shifting from the simple nomadic life prevalent in the peninsula to an urban and sophisticated one. Contacts with Greece and Persia gave a greater impulse to music, which frequently accompanied the recitation of prose and poetry. By the mid-800's in the Baghdad capital of Abbassids under Harun al-Rashid and al-Ma'mun, Islamic culture as well as commerce and contacts with many other parts of the world flourished.

In the fourth century B.C., when Alexander the Great conquered Asia Minor and founded Alexandria, he set the stage for the great migration of Greek philosophy and science to that part of the world. During the Ptolemaic period, Alexandria, Egypt, was the radiant center for the development and spread of Greek culture throughout the Mediterranean. That great center of learning continued after 641, when Egypt became part of the Muslim state. Thereafter Syria, Baghdad, and Persia became similar channels for the communication of essentially Greek, Syriac, pre-Islamic Persian and Indian cultural values. As a result, Islamic philosophy was influenced by the writings of Socrates, Plato, and Aristotle. The great Muslim philosophers such as Ibn Khaldun (d. 1406), Ibn Sina (Avicenna, d. 1037), Ibn Rushd (Averroes, d. 1198), al-Farabi and al-Ghazali translated the works of earlier Greek philosophers and added their own significant contributions. It was essentially through such works, intellectually faithful to the originals, that Western civilization was able to benefit from these earlier legacies. In fact, St. Thomas Aquinas, the founder of Catholic naturalism, developed his views of Aristotle through the translation of Ibn Sina (Avicenna) and Ibn Rushd (Averroes). These great philosophers produced a wealth of new ideas that enriched civilization, particularly Western civilization which has depended so much on their works. The influence of Islam ultimately made possible the European Renaissance, which was generated by the ideas of the Greeks filtered through the Muslim philosophers.

The same is true of early legal writings of Muslim scholars such as al-Shaybani, who in the seventh century started the case method of teaching Islamic international law that was subsequently put into writing in the twelfth century by a disciple in India. It was the basis for the writings of the legal canonists of the fifteenth and sixteenth centuries on certain aspects of international law, in particular the laws of war and peace.

The study of history held a particular fascination for Arab Muslims imbued with a sense of mission. Indeed, because Islam is a religion for all peoples and all times, and because the *Qur'an* states that God created the universe and caused it to be inhabited by men and women and peoples and tribes so that they may know each other, there was a quest for discovery and knowledge. As a result Muslims recorded their own history and that of others. But they added insight to facts and gave to events, people, and places a philosophical dimension expressed in the universal history written by al-Tabari of Baghdad (838-923). In the introduction to his multi-volume work he devoted an entire volume to the science of history and its implications. Al-Tabari also wrote an authoritative text on the history of prophets and kings which continues to be a most comprehensive record of the period from Abraham to the tenth century.

The West's fascination with Arabo-Islamic culture can be seen in many ways. "The Thousand and One Nights" captured Western Europe's cultural and popular fancy in the 1700's (first translated into French by Galland in 1704, then into English). Dante's "Divine Comedy" contains reference to the Prophet's ascension to Heaven. Shakespeare in "Othello" and the "Merchant of Venice" describes Moorish subjects. Victor Hugo writes of Persians as do Boccaccio and Chaucer. Even "Robinson Crusoe" and "Gulliver's Tales" are adaptations of "The Thousand and One Nights." Arabo-Islamic culture, knowledge, scholarship, and science fed the Western world's development for five hundred years between the tenth and fifteenth centuries.

The Sciences

From the second half of the eighth century to the end of the eleventh century, Islamic scientific developments were the basis of knowledge in the world. At a period of history when the scientific and philosophical heritage of the ancient world was about to be lost, Islamic scholars stepped in to preserve that heritage from destruction. Indeed, without the cultivation of science in these early centuries by Islamic scholars, it is probable that texts which later exercised a formative influence over Western culture would never have survived intact. It is certain, moreover, that the modern world would look much different than it does today. For the culture and civilization that were founded on Islam not only preserved the heritage of the ancient world but codified, systematized, explained, criticized, modified, and, finally, built on past contributions in the process of making distinctive contributions of their own.

The story of Islam's role in the preservation and transmission of ancient science, to say nothing of its own lasting contributions, is truly fascinating—and a bit of a puzzle. Why is it that so many ancient Greek texts survive only in Arabic translations? How did the Arabs, who had no direct contact with the science and learning of the Greeks, come to be the inheritors of the classical tradition?

The answers to these questions are to be found in a unique conjunction of historical forces. From the first, it appears, the Umayyad dynasty located in Damascus evinced an interest in things Greek, for they employed educated Greek-speaking civil servants extensively.

Page from the treatise in Arabic on farming "al-Filaha al-Nabatiyyah" by Ibn Wahshiyyah. It deals with popular customs and religion and also contains agricultural and botanical informations. (Bodleian Library, Oxford, England).

Early friezes on mosques from the period show a familiarity with the astrological lore of late antiquity.

The theory of numbers, developed and expanded from the original Indian contribution, resulted in the "Arabic numbers" 1 through 9. Islamic scholars also used the concept of zero, which was a Hindu concept. Without the zero, neither mathematics, algebra, nor cybernetics would have developed. Algebra was essentially developed by the Arab Muslims; the very word derives from the Arabic *al-jabr*. Among the most prominent scholars is the Basra born Ibn al-Haytham (965-1030), who developed the "Alhazen problem," one of the basic algebraic problems, and who made great contributions to optics and physics. He had advanced long before Newton the thesis that extraterrestrial scientific phenomena governed the motion of the earth and stars. He also developed experiments on light which were nothing short of extraordinary at that time. He demonstrated the theory of parallels, based on the finding that light travels in straight lines, and the passing of light through glass. Astronomy, developed by the Babylonians, continued to flourish under Islam. It soon expanded beyond the science of observation into the design of measuring instruments. In addition, it gave rise to the development of planetary theory.

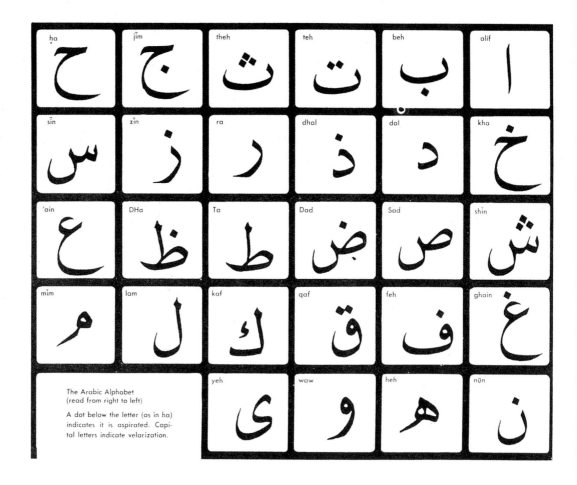

The Arabic Alphabet
(read from right to left)

A dot below the letter (as in ha) indicates it is aspirated. Capital letters indicate velarization.

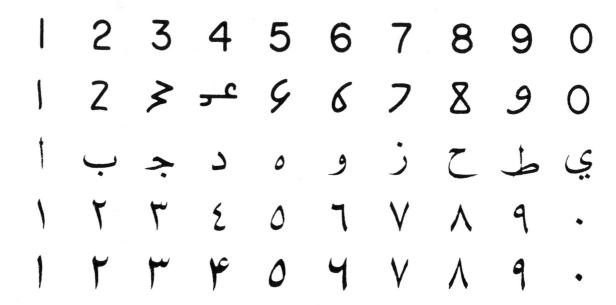

The medical sciences were largely developed throughout the works of Ibn Sina (Avicenna), al-Razzi, and Husayn bin Ishak al-Ibadi, who translated Hippocrates and other Greeks. Razi (860-940) is reported to have written 200 books on medicine, one of them on medical ethics, and the *Hawi*, a 25 volume practical encyclopedia. Ibn Sina (980-1037) became a famed physician at 18 who wrote 16 books and the *Canoun*, an encyclopedia on all known diseases in the world. It was translated into many languages. But medical science soon led into zoology, veterinary medicine, pharmacy, pharmacology and chemistry. Indeed the word "chemistry" derives from the Arabic word al-kemia or alchemy as it was later known. The most important medical school was that of Judishapur, Iran, which after 738 became part of the Muslim world. It was managed by Syrian Christians and became the center for most Muslim practical learning and the model for the hospitals built under the Abbasids (between 749-1258).

The Arabs clearly followed the *Hadith* of the Prophet urging them to pursue knowledge from birth to death, even if that search was to be in China (deemed the most remote place on the earth.)

The Abbasids, who displaced the Umayyads and moved the seat of government from Damascus to Baghdad, made the first serious effort to accommodate Greek science and philosophy to Islam. The Abbasid rulers, unlike the Umayyads who remained Arab in their tastes and customs, conceived an Islamic polity based on religious affiliation rather than nationality or race. This made it easier for people of differing cultural, racial, and intellectual heritages to mingle and exchange ideas as equals. Persian astronomers from Gandeshapur could work side by side with mathematicians from Alexandria in the cosmopolitan atmosphere of Baghdad.

Then, too, the success of the Islamic conquest had erased existing national boundaries which had worked to keep peoples linguistically, politically, and intellectually apart. For the first time since Alexander the Great former rivals could meet and exchange ideas under the protection of a single state. The rise of Arabic as the international language of science and government administration helped matters along. As the cultivation of the sciences intensified and the high civilization of the Abbasids blossomed, the expressive resources of Arabic blossomed as well, soon making Arabic the language of choice for international commerce and scholarship as well as divine revelation.

Most important of all, however, it was the attitude that developed within the Islamic state toward the suspect writings of the Greeks. Unlike the Christian communities of late antiquity, whose attitudes toward the pagan philosophers were shaped by the experience of Roman persecution, Muslims did not suffer—or at least to the same degree—the conflict between faith and reason. On the contrary, the *Qur'an* enjoined Muslims to seek knowledge all their lives, no matter what the source or where it might lead. As a result, Muslims of the Abbasid period quickly set about recovering the scientific and philosophical works of the classical past—lying neglected in the libraries of Byzantium—and translating them into Arabic.

The task was herculean and complicated by the fact that texts of the classical period could not be translated directly from Greek into Arabic. Rather, they had first to be rendered in Syriac, the language with which Christian translators were most familiar, and then translated into Arabic by native speakers. This circuitous route was made necessary by the fact that Christian communities, whose language was Syriac, tended to know Greek, whereas Muslims generally found it easier to learn Syriac, which is closer to Arabic.

The translation effort began in earnest under the reign of the second Abbasid caliph, al-Mansur (754-75). He sent emissaries to the Byzantine emperor requesting mathematical texts and received in response a copy of Euclid's *Elements.* This single gift, more than any

other perhaps, ignited a passion for learning that was to last throughout the golden age of Islam and beyond. The effort was subsequently systematized under al-Ma'mun, who founded an institution expressly for the purpose, called the *Bait al-Hikmah* or House of Wisdom, which was staffed with salaried Muslim and Christian scholars. The output of the House of Wisdom over the centuries was prodigious, encompassing as it did nearly the entire corpus of the Greek scientific and philosophical thought. Not only Euclid but Aristotle, Galen and Hippocrates, and Archimedes were among the authors to receive early treatment.

It would be wrong to suggest that the scholars of the House of Wisdom were occupied with task of translation only. Muslim scholars generally were concerned to understand, codify, correct, and, most importantly, assimilate the learning of the ancients to the conceptual framework of Islam. The greatest of these scholars were original and systematic thinkers of the first order, like the great Arab philosopher al-Farabi who died in 950. His *Catalog of Sciences* had a tremendous effect on the curricula of medieval universities.

Perhaps the most distinctive and noteworthy contributions occurred in the field of mathematics, where scholars from the House of Wisdom played a critical role in fusing the Indian and classical traditions, thus inaugurating the great age of Islamic mathematical speculation. The first great advance consisted in the introduction of Arabic numerals—which, as far as can be determined, were Indian in origin. They embody the "place-value" theory, which permits numbers to be expressed by nine figures plus zero. This development not only simplified calculation but paved the way for the development of an entirely new branch of mathematics, algebra.

The study of geometry was sustained by a remarkable series of scholars, the *Banu Musa* or "Sons of Musa," who were all, quite literally, sons of the al-Ma'mun's court astronomer, Musa ibn Shakir. Their activities were all the more noteworthy because they carried on their research and writing as private citizens, devoting their lives and expending their fortunes in the pursuit of knowledge. Not only did they sponsor the translation of numerous Greek works but contributed substantial works of their own. Al-Hasan, one of the sons, was perhaps the foremost geometrician of his time, translating six books of the *Elements* and working out the remainder of the proofs on his own.

The enormous intellectual energy unleashed by the Abbasid dynasty left no field of knowledge and speculation untouched. In addition to mathematics and geometry, Abbasid scholars in the House of Wisdom

Arabic Words That Entered the Western Vocabulary

AL-JABR = ALGEBRA
AL-KEMIA = CHEMISTRY
AL-KUHL = ALCOHOL
AL-MIRAL = ADMIRAL
AL'UD = LUTE
'ANBAR = AMBER
BAWRAQ = BORAX
GHARBALA = GARBLE
GHOL = GHOUL
LAYMUN = LEMON
MAKHZAN = MAGASIN (French)
NARANJ = ORANGE
QAHWAH = COFFEE, CAFE
QANAH = CANE
QITAR = GUITAR
SAFARA = SAFARI
SUKKAR = SUGAR = ASUKAR (Spanish)
TAFRIK = TRAFFIC
TA'RIF = TARIFF
TUNBAR = TAMBOURINE = TAMBOUR (French)
ZIRAFAH = GIRAFFE

made important and lasting contributions in astronomy, ethics, mechanics, music, medicine, physics, and philosophy to name a few. In the process men of enormous intellect and productivity rose to prominence. One of these was Thabit ibn Qurra. Recruited from the provinces—where he had worked in obscurity as a money changer—he came to the *Bait al-Hikmah* to work as a translator. There his exemplary grasp of Syriac, Greek, and Arabic made him invaluable. In addition to his translations of key works, such as Archimedes' *Measurement of the Circle* (later translated into Latin by Gerard of Cremona in the 12th century), he also wrote over 70 original works on a wide range of subjects. His sons, too, were to found a dynasty of scholars that lasted until the 10th century.

But it wasn't only the pure or abstract sciences that received emphasis in these early years. The practical and technical arts made advances as well, medicine the first among them. Here several great scholars deserve mention. Hunain ibn Ishaq not only translated the entire canon of Greek medical works into Arabic—including the Hippocratic oath, obligatory for doctors then as now—but wrote 29 works by his own pen, the most important a collection of ten essays on ophthalmology. The greatest of the 9th century physician-philosophers was perhaps Abu Bakr Muhammad ibn Zakariya al-Razi, known to the west as Rhazes. He wrote over 184 books and was an early advocate of experiment and observation in science.

Simultaneously, in far off Spain *(al-Andalus),* the social and natural sciences were being advanced by men such as Ibn Khaldun, the first historian to explicate the laws governing the rise and fall of civilizations. The brilliant flowering of Islamic science in Andalusia was directly stimulated by the renaissance in Baghdad. Scholars regularly traveled the length of the known world to sit and learn at the feet of a renowned teacher.

With the death of the philosopher al-Farabi in 950 the first and most brilliant period of Islamic scientific thought drew to a close. As the political empire fragmented over the next 300 years, leadership would pass to the provinces, principally Khorasan and Andalusia. Indeed, Spain was to serve as a conduit through which the learning of the ancient world, augmented and transformed by the Islamic experience, was to pass to

medieval Europe and the modern world. At the very time that Baghdad fell to the Mongols in 1258, and the Abbasid caliphate came to an end, scribes in Europe were preserving the Muslim scientific tradition. This is why, just as many Greek texts now survive only in Arabic dress, many Arabic scientific works only survive in Latin.

The death of al-Farabi is perhaps a fitting event to mark the end of the golden age of Muslim science. His masterwork, *The Perfect City,* exemplifies the extent to which Greek culture and science had been successfully and productively assimilated and then impressed with the indelible stamp of Islam. The perfect city, in al-Farabi's view, is founded on moral and ethical principles; from these flow its perfect shape and physical infrastructure. Undoubtedly he had in mind the round city of Baghdad, The City of Peace.

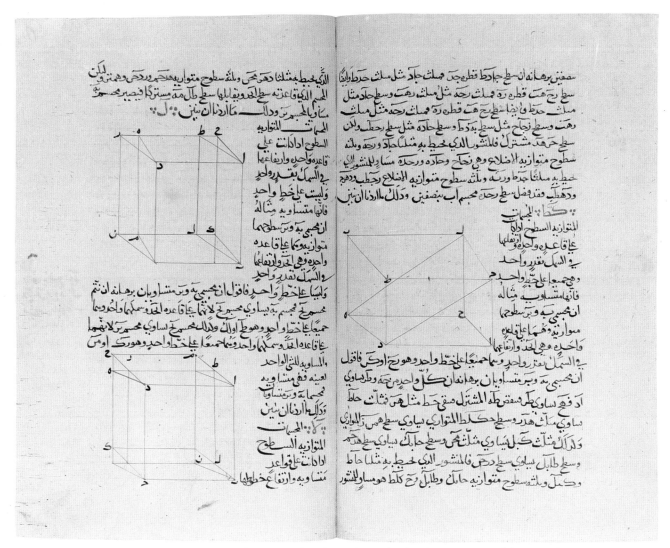

Page from one of the six books of Euclid's Elements translated into the Arabic by al-Hassan one of the sons of Musa, in the 9th century. (Bodleian Library, Oxford, England.)

Trade and Commerce as a Cultural Vehicle

Because Arabs historically had a tradition of trade and commerce, the Muslims continued that tradition. It was due to their superiority in navigation, shipbuilding, astronomy, and scientific measuring devices that Arab and Muslim commerce and trade developed and reached so many peoples throughout the world. The Arabs were at the crossroads of the ancient trade routes from the Mediterranean, the Arabian Gulf, East Africa, and the Indian subcontinent, all the way to China.

One of the interesting results of these trading relations occurred during the caliphate of Harun al-Rashid (786-809) when he exchanged envoys and gifts with Charlemagne, the Holy Roman Emperor. As a result, Harun al-Rashid established the Christian Pilgrims' Inn in Jerusalem, fulfilling Umar's pledge to Bishop Sophronious, when he first entered Jerusalem, to allow freedom of religion and access to Jerusalem to Christian religious pilgrims.

A number of Arabic words relating to the trade and commerce have found their way into modern Western languages. (See list of words.) Muslin cotton developed in Mosul (Iraq) became a favorite commodity and a new word in the Western vocabulary, as did damask fabric (from Damascus), fustain cloth (from Fustat, Egypt).

The most interesting accounts of other cultures encountered by Arab Muslims are contained in a book on the travels of Ibn Battutah of Tangier (1304-1377), who over a period of 25 years traveled to Asia Minor, Mongolia, Russia, China, the Maldives, Southeast Asia and Africa and recounted his travels and the influence of early Muslim traders in those regions. He was the precursor of Marco Polo, whose accounts contained detailed descriptions of various cultures with which Arab and Muslims traders had long been in contact. Islamic craftsmanship in bookmaking and bookbinding were items of trade which carried the message of Islamic civilization far and wide.

Architecture and music

The word "Arabesque" entered into the Western lexicon as a description of the intricate design that characterized Arab Muslim art. But the great mosques that were first built throughout the Islamic world were not only places of worship but places of learning which remained as great examples of architecture and design. Through them civilization was transmitted in an artistic environment that was at once intellectually inspiring and emotionally uplifting. The Haram Mosque of Mecca, the Mosque of Al-Aqsa in Jerusalem, the numerous mosques in Cairo—Al-Azhar, Amr, Sultan Hassan, Baybars—the Great Umayyad Mosque of Damascus, the Quairawan in Tunisia, the Blue Mosque in Istanbul, the Cordoba Mosque in Spain and the Kutubiyah in Marakesh are among the most noteworthy. In addition to distinctive architectural characteristics, such as magnificent geometric designs, many of these contain mosaics of rare beauty, frequently painted in the blue and green of the sea, sky, and vegetation. The wood carving (*masharabiyah*) in most mosques are equally distinctive and characteristic of Islamic art.

At times of prayer, individuals and congregations—indeed the entire Muslim world—face Mecca. The mosque is usually a domed structure with one or more minarets from which the *muadhin* gives the call to prayer five times a day. The direction of Mecca is clearly indicated by the *mihrab,* a decorated niche in the wall. The larger mosques have a *minbar* or pulpit. Since the worshipers should be in a pure state of mind and body before they begin to pray, a fountain is placed in the courtyard for ritual ablutions. Shoes are removed on entering the prayer hall, which is usually carpeted.

For Muslims the mosque is a place for worship and education, a refuge from the cares of the world. Its function is best described in the Prophet's own words, namely that the mosque should be a garden of paradise. Islam's greatest architect was Sinan, a 16th century Ottoman builder who was responsible for the Sulaimaniye mosque in Istanbul. His mosques visibly display the discipline, might, and splendor of Islam.

The most notable examples of *masharabiyah* are in the Mosque of Ibn Tulun in Cairo, the Blue Mosque in Istanbul, and the Mosque of Isfahan. After the *Ka'ba* in Mecca, the "Dome of the Rock" or Mosque of Umar in Jerusalem built in 685 is the oldest example of Muslim architectural genius. The technique of dome construction was perfected and passed on to the West. The technique of dome structural support was used in the Capella Palatine in Palermo (1132), while the campaniles or steeples of the Palazzo Vecchio of Florence and of San Marco in Venice are inspired by the minaret which was first built in Qairawan, Tunisia (670). Similarly, the horseshoe arch, which was so prevalent in Islamic form and particularly well realized in the Great Mosque of Damascus (707), has since been copied all over the world. Probably the best known example of Islamic architecture is the Alhambra (meaning al- Hamra or the red one) palace built in 1230 in Granada, Spain.

But artistic contributions were not limited to architecture, construction, decoration, painting, mosaic, calligraphy, design, metalcraft and wood carving. They extended to music through the development of new instruments and new techniques of sound and rhythm. The Arab Muslims (al-Farabi in particular) were the first to develop a technique of musical harmony paralleling mathematical science. Arabic-Islamic music was characterized by the harmony of sound and evocative emotional expression. *Musiqa* is the Arabic word for music.

Page from the Automata showing the servants basin, which was a device for washing. Mamluk period, 14th century, Egypt. (Aramco World Magazine, November/December 1981; photo by Steve Earley.)

Islamic Fundamentalism

Many non-Muslims perceive Islamic Fundamentalism as a form of revolutionary ideology and associate it with groups and movements which engage in violent acts or advocate violence. This must be distinguished from Islamic revival which is a peaceful movement calling for the return to basic traditional values and practices. Adherents to and followers of such a movement believe that the best way to achieve the "true path of Islam" is to develop an integrated social and political system based on Islamic ideals and the teachings of the *Qur'an* and the *Sunna.* To that extent they are fundamentalists.

Reform ideas which derive from revival movements are not new to the history of Islam, nor do they advocate resorting to violence in order to achieve such a goal except where rebellion against unjust rule is legally justified. Examples of peaceful reform ideas are found in the learned teachings of the 13th century philosopher-scholar Ibn Taymiyya in Syria. In the 18th century the Wahabi reform movement developed in Saudi Arabia and its orthodox teachings continue to the present. Also in the 19th century the ideal of the "true path to justice" or *al-salaf al-salih* was eloquently propounded by Sheik Muhammad Abduh in Egypt, and his views continue to be studied by religious and secular scholars all over the world. These and other reform ideas have in common the search for Islamic truth and justice and their applicability to the solutions to Muslim societies' problems.

Because Islam is a holistic religion integrating all aspects of life, it follows that a reform movement predicated on religion necessarily confronts the social, economic, and political realities of the society in which it develops. Muslim societies, however, have emerged from colonialism and neo-colonialism and are seeking to develop free from certain western influences which may corrupt or subvert basic Islamic values. Furthermore in Islam there is no division or distinction between what in the West is called "Church and State". In fact westerners refer to the Islamic form of government as a theocracy. Thus contemporary political-religious groups focus on social, political, and economic aspects of Muslim societies. They oppose the secular state and instead call for the establishment of a "Muslim State".

A distinction must be made between Islamic reform and Islamic political activism conducted under the banner of Islam. The latter is sometimes characterized by extremism, fanaticism, and violence, which are contrary to Islamic precepts. But these manifestations of a socio-political nature must not be confused with the ideals and values of Islam.

Enlightened reform ideas continue to develop in the Muslim world. Institutions like Al-Azhar University in Cairo, which is the oldest university in the world, the Muslim World League in Mecca, and the Organization of the Islamic Conference headquartered in Jeddah are the examples of the contemporary, intellectual, educational, and diplomatic forces in the resurgence of Islam. The contributions they make toward a better understanding of Islam, as well as its peaceful propagation, are free from extremism and violence.

The resurgence of Islam is flourishing in every part of the world and dedicated Muslims are trying hard to meet the challenges of modern times while remaining faithful to the values of their past. This is enlightened Islamic Fundamentalism. Its continuation and growth are ongoing. But since all mass movements carry the risk of excess, extremism by some is likely to occur at times. However, one should not judge the higher values shared by the many on the basis of the extreme deeds committed by the few.

Jamaat Mosque at Ruimveldt, outside George-town, Guyana. (Aramco World Magazine.)

Traditional houses, Jakarta, Indonesia. (Consulate of Indonesia, Chicago.)

Yaama Mosque in Yaama, Niger, completed in 1982. Recipient of the 1986 Aga Khan Award. (Aga Khan Award; photo by Kamran Adle.)

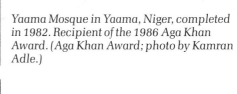

Bhong Mosque in Bhong, Pakistan, completed in 1982. Recipient of the 1986 Aga Khan Award. (Aga Khan Award; photo by Jacques Betant.)

The present and the future

Muslims, irrespective of whether they come from the Arab world, Africa, Asia Minor, Central Asia, China, the Soviet Union or Western societies, still feel strongly united in their shared beliefs and values. Muslims believe that they have a contribution to make in this world, either as individuals or as a community, and that their behavior and demeanor can set an example to others. In Muslim countries the problems, dilemmas, and frustrations are numerous. With the gradual disintegration of the Muslim state, beginning in the twelfth century, many of the countries fell under foreign rule for extensive periods of time, Ottoman Turkish domination for some at first, and then European colonialism. They have had to make up for many years during which their economic, social, and cultural development was blunted by both external and internal causes. To do so they have to struggle not only against problems of underdevelopment but also forces of rapid change.

The search for an Islamic way is ongoing throughout the Muslim world. It is an uneasy search seeking to link the fundamentals of a glorious past with a future that offers only hopeful promises dimmed by present difficulties. Most Muslims as individuals are undaunted, for every Muslim believes that he has to act during his lifetime as if he will live forever. He has a sense of permanence and continuity, knowing that the work begun by one person will be carried on by another. There is a constant hope for a better tomorrow; but then, what counts is the hereafter. Ours is not to insure a result but to try our best to achieve it in the right way. However, the end does not justify the means. The moral-ethical dimension of conduct and method must always predominate.

The challenge of Islam is a challenge to all Muslim societies: to create the types of economic, social, and political institutions that will preserve the basic ethical and moral values of Islam together with the individual freedom of every Muslim. This involves achieving a delicate balance between the needs of the community and the right of the individual to the full attainment of freedom, equality, justice and what under the U.S. Constitution is called "the pursuit of happiness." This also is a legitimate goal in Islam, as set forth by the tenth century Muslim philosopher—the mathematician al-Farabi. A significant part of his major text on truth is devoted to the attainment of happiness.

Top left, modern Water Tower in Kuwait. (Embassy of Kuwait, Washington, D.C.)

Bottom left,   Soldier Monument in Baghdad, Iraq. (Embassy of Iraq, Washington, D.C.)

Top right, mosque in Northbrook, Illinois, U.S.A. (Muslim Community Centre in Chicago)

Bottom right, contemporary Picture showing a view of Dar al-Islam village in New Mexico. (Dar al-Islam village, New Mexico.)

"Everyone of you is a shepherd, and everyone of you will be questioned about those under his rule: The Amir is a shepherd and he will be questioned about his subjects, the man is a ruler in his family and he will be questioned about those under his care; and the woman is a ruler in the house of her husband and she will be questioned about those under her care."
The Prophet's Hadith.

٦، يَبُنَىَّ أَقِمِ الصَّلٰوةَ وَأۡمُرۡ بِالۡمَعۡرُوۡفِ وَانۡهَ عَنِ الۡمُنۡكَرِ وَاصۡبِرۡ عَلٰى مَاۤ أَصَابَكَۚ إِنَّ ذٰلِكَ مِنۡ عَزۡمِ الۡأُمُوۡرِ

O my son!
Observe your
prayers, order
(enjoin or com-
mand) with what
is just (right and
fair) and admon-
ish (forbid) what
is wrong; and bear
with patience on
what befalls upon
you; for this is
determination of
purpose.

Qur'an 31:17

بسم الله الرحمن الرحيم

اليوم اكملت لكم دينكم واتممت عليكم نعمتي ورضيت لكم الاسلام دينا

صدق الله العظيم

This day have I perfected your religion for you, completed my favour upon you, and have chosen for you Islam as your religion.

Qur'an 5:4

About the Author

M. Cherif Bassiouni

Professor of Law, DePaul University, since 1964; 1970 Fulbright-Hays Professor of International Criminal Law, The University of Freiburg, Germany; 1971 Visiting Professor of Law, N.Y.U.; 1972 Guest Scholar Woodrow Wilson International Center for Scholars, Washington, D.C. He is non-resident Dean of The International Institute of Higher Studies in Criminal Sciences (Siracusa, Italy) since 1976.

He studied law in the three major legal systems of the world: civil law, common law, and Islamic *Sharia*, at Dijon University, France, The University of Geneva Switzerland, and the University of Cairo, Egypt. His degrees are: J.D., Indiana University; LL.M., John Marshall Law School; S.J.D., George Washington University. In 1981 he was awarded the degree: Doctor of Law *Honoris causa* (Dottore in Giurisprudenza) from the University of Torino, Italy, and in 1988, the degree: Doctor of Law *Honoris causa* (Docteur d'Etat en Droit) conferred at The University of Pau, France.

He is the author of twenty-two books on U.S. Criminal Law and International and comparative Criminal Law and over 100 law review articles.

Active in several scholarly and professional organizations, he has served as the Secretary-General of the International Association of Penal Law since 1974; chairman of the International Law Section of the Illinois State Bar Association for several years, and chairman of several committees of the Chicago Bar and American Bar Associations.

A frequent lecturer at distinguished universities in the U.S. and abroad, he has also been a frequent U.N.consultant: Fifth U.N. Congress on Crime Prevention (1975) where he was elected Honorary Vice-President of the Congress; Sixth U.N. Congress (1980) where he presented a Draft International Criminal Code; U.N. Division of Human Rights in 1980-1981 for which he prepared a Draft Statute for the Creation of an International Criminal Court; Seventh U.N. Congress, for which he chaired two preparatory meetings of committees of experts in 1983-1984. He also served in 1978 as co-chairman of the committee of experts which prepared the U.N. Draft Convention of the Prevention and Suppression of Torture, and chairman of the committee of experts which prepared the U.N. Draft Convention on the Prevention of Unlawful Human Experimentation.

He was also a consultant to the Departments of State and Justice on projects relating to international traffic in drugs (1973) and control of terrorism (1975 and 1978) and the defense of the U.S. hostages in Iran (1979).

Among the distinctions and awards he received are: 1956, Order of Merit, Egypt; 1977, Order of Merit, Italy (Rank of Commendatore); 1978, Order of Merit, Italy, (Rank of Grand' Ufficiale); 1984, Order of Sciences, Egypt), (Rank of First Class). Also among others: 1967, Outstanding Citizen of the Year of Metropolitan Chicago; 1970, Outstanding Educator of America; 1973, Gold Medal of the Italian Press (Rome, Italy).

He has been admitted to practice in Illinois and Washington, D.C. and before the United States Supreme Court, the Second, Fifth, Seventh, and Eleventh Circuits of the U.S. Courts of Appeals, the United States Court of Military Appeals, and the United States Court of International Trade.

Since 1973 he has served as member of the Board and President of the MidAmerica Arab Chamber of Commerce.